School
Violence

Other Books of Related Interest

School
Violence

Bryan J. Grapes, *Book Editor*

David L. Bender, *Publisher*
Bruno Leone, *Executive Editor*
Bonnie Szumski, *Editorial Director*
David M. Haugen, *Managing Editor*
Brenda Stalcup, *Series Editor*

Contemporary Issues
Companion

Greenhaven Press, Inc., San Diego, CA

Every effort has been made to trace the owners of copyrighted material. The articles in this volume may have been edited for content, length, and/or reading level. The titles have been changed to enhance the editorial purpose. Those interested in locating the original source will find the complete citation on the first page of each article.

Library of Congress Cataloging-in-Publication Data

School violence / Bryan J. Grapes, book editor
    p.   cm. — (Contemporary issues companion)
    Includes bibliographical references and index.
    ISBN 0-7377-0332-6 (lib. bdg. : alk. paper). —
ISBN 0-7377-0331-8 (pbk. : alk. paper)
    1. School violence—United States. I. Grapes, Bryan J., 1970– .
II. Series.

LB3013.3 .S376 2000
371.7'82—dc21   99-058905
                                         CIP

©2000 by Greenhaven Press, Inc.
P.O. Box 289009, San Diego, CA 92198-9009

Printed in the U.S.A.

CONTENTS

FOREWORD

In the news, on the streets, and in neighborhoods, individuals are confronted with a variety of social problems. Such problems may affect people directly: A young woman may struggle with depression, suspect a friend of having bulimia, or watch a loved one battle cancer. And even the issues that do not directly affect her private life—such as religious cults, domestic violence, or legalized gambling—still impact the larger society in which she lives. Discovering and analyzing the complexities of issues that encompass communal and societal realms as well as the world of personal experience is a valuable educational goal in the modern world.

Effectively addressing social problems requires familiarity with a constantly changing stream of data. Becoming well informed about today's controversies is an intricate process that often involves reading myriad primary and secondary sources, analyzing political debates, weighing various experts' opinions—even listening to first-hand accounts of those directly affected by the issue. For students and general observers, this can be a daunting task because of the sheer volume of information available in books, periodicals, on the evening news, and on the Internet. Researching the consequences of legalized gambling, for example, might entail sifting through congressional testimony on gambling's societal effects, examining private studies on Indian gaming, perusing numerous websites devoted to Internet betting, and reading essays written by lottery winners as well as interviews with recovering compulsive gamblers. Obtaining valuable information can be time-consuming—since it often requires researchers to pore over numerous documents and commentaries before discovering a source relevant to their particular investigation.

Greenhaven's Contemporary Issues Companion series seeks to assist this process of research by providing readers with useful and pertinent information about today's complex issues. Each volume in this anthology series focuses on a topic of current interest, presenting informative and thought-provoking selections written from a wide variety of viewpoints. The readings selected by the editors include such diverse sources as personal accounts and case studies, pertinent factual and statistical articles, and relevant commentaries and overviews. This diversity of sources and views, found in every Contemporary Issues Companion, offers readers a broad perspective in one convenient volume.

In addition, each title in the Contemporary Issues Companion series is designed especially for young adults. The selections included in every volume are chosen for their accessibility and are expertly edited in consideration of both the reading and comprehension levels of the audience. The structure of the anthologies also enhances accessibility. An introductory essay places each issue in context and provides helpful facts such as historical background or current statistics and legislation that pertain to the topic. The chapters that follow organize the material and focus on specific aspects of the book's topic. Every essay is introduced by a brief summary of its main points and biographical information about the author. These summaries aid in comprehension and can also serve to direct readers to material of immediate interest and need. Finally, a comprehensive index allows readers to efficiently scan and locate content.

The Contemporary Issues Companion series is an ideal launching point for research on a particular topic. Each anthology in the series is composed of readings taken from an extensive gamut of resources, including periodicals, newspapers, books, government documents, the publications of private and public organizations, and Internet websites. In these volumes, readers will find factual support suitable for use in reports, debates, speeches, and research papers. The anthologies also facilitate further research, featuring a book and periodical bibliography and a list of organizations to contact for additional information.

A perfect resource for both students and the general reader, Greenhaven's Contemporary Issues Companion series is sure to be a valued source of current, readable information on social problems that interest young adults. It is the editors' hope that readers will find the Contemporary Issues Companion series useful as a starting point to formulate their own opinions about and answers to the complex issues of the present day.

INTRODUCTION

On April 20, 1999, Eric Harris and Dylan Klebold entered Columbine High School in Littleton, Colorado, firing sawed-off shotguns and tossing homemade pipe bombs at their fellow students. Twelve classmates and one teacher were killed and twenty-three students were wounded before Harris and Klebold turned their guns on themselves. Exacerbating the grief and fear that arose in the wake of the shooting in Littleton is the fact that it is only one of a growing list of similar school shootings that have taken place across America.

In addition to the massacre at Columbine, eight other mass shootings have occurred in U.S. schools between 1996 and 1999. On February 2, 1996, Barry Loukaitis killed two students and one teacher and wounded one student at his school in Moses Lake, Washington. Evan Ramsey shot and killed one teacher and one classmate in his Bethel, Alaska, high school on February 19, 1997. In Pearl, Mississippi, Luke Woodham killed two classmates and wounded seven others at his high school on October 1, 1997. On December 1, 1997, Michael Carneal shot and killed three students and wounded five others at Heath High School in West Paducah, Kentucky. Mitchell Johnson and Andrew Golden killed one teacher and four students and wounded ten others at Westside Middle School in Jonesboro, Arkansas, on March 24, 1998. Andrew Wurst opened fire at a school dance in Edinboro, Pennsylvania, on April 24, 1998, killing one teacher and wounding two classmates. On May 21, 1998, Kip Kinkel shot and killed two students and wounded twenty-two others at Thurston High School in Springfield, Oregon. And on May 20, 1999, exactly one month after the massacre at Columbine, T.J. Solomon opened fire on his classmates in a crowded hallway at Heritage High School in Conyers, Georgia, wounding six.

Despite the staggering casualties from this string of mass shootings—thirty-five dead and seventy-six wounded—statistics indicate that violence in American schools is actually becoming less frequent. A study published in the *Journal of the American Medical Association* on August 4, 1999, determined that "between 1991 and 1997, U.S. high school students became less likely to carry weapons, to engage in physical fights, and to be injured in physical fights." Statistics gathered by writers Jerry Adler and Karen Springen in the May 3, 1999, edition of *Newsweek* indicate that a high school senior is two hundred times as likely to be admitted to Harvard as to be killed in his or her school. According to a 1998 report by the U.S. Departments of Justice and Education, the probability of a child getting struck by lightning is one in a million, yet this chance is greater than that of a child being murdered on school grounds. Nevertheless, the string of high-profile school shootings has generated significant anxiety in most communities and inspired many school boards to closely examine campus safety. Consequently, a number of schools have dramatically increased the level of security on school grounds in an effort to avoid another Littleton. Metal detectors, armed security guards, drug- and bomb-sniffing dogs, blast-proof doors and windows, razor-wire fences, frequent searches of lockers and students' personal belongings, and a heightened sensitivity to threatening language, unique clothing and hairstyles, and antisocial behavior are all becoming commonplace in U.S. schools.

Some school officials and students feel that the heightened security measures are necessary to establish the school administration's authority and to ensure that students have a safe learning environment. "We've got to let the kids know who's in charge of the schools," argues Michael E. Sumner, chairman of the Coweta County school board in Georgia. "And if that means we're infringing on somebody's individual freedom of expression, then so be it." Flynn K. Tracy, valedictorian of the class of 1999 at Newnan High School in Newnan, Georgia, agrees: "Whether they take minor steps or major steps, schools should do anything they can to make themselves safer."

However, many observers feel that the measures being adopted by some schools are too extreme. Critics argue that many of the heightened security policies represent a panicked overreaction to a handful of isolated incidents. As evidence of overzealous enforcement of safety precautions, critics point to a list of students who have been arrested or suspended for nothing more than an off-color remark or for submitting a writing assignment with dark themes. For instance, a student in Virginia was suspended in 1999 after writing a fictional essay about a student who had a nuclear weapon strapped to his chest. During a classroom discussion of the Littleton massacre, a fourteen-year-old girl in Harrisburg, Pennsylvania, said that she could understand how ostracized students might turn homicidal: This comment led to her being strip-searched and suspended for two weeks.

Critics of such harsh measures warn that introducing a police-state atmosphere in the classroom could have adverse effects on students. According to columnist Stephen Chapman, "Turning schools into replicas of medium-security prisons is excellent preparation for living in North Korea, but it is not a good way to develop responsible citizens fit for a free society." Chapman explains that "seeing a threat in every backpack or funny hairstyle is a symptom of irrational panic, not sensible caution."

A primary contributing factor to the sense of panic felt by many parents and school officials is the location in which these massacres have taken place. All nine of the high-profile school shootings between 1996 and 1999 occurred at rural or suburban schools in affluent neighborhoods. Violence in inner-city schools is not a new phenomenon. Since the explosion of the crack cocaine trade in the 1980s, drug- and gang-related violence in inner-city schools has reflected the grim conditions found in many inner-city neighborhoods. But most residents of suburban and rural America believed the violence that plagued inner-city schools could not possibly be transported to the quiet, tree-lined streets of a town like Littleton. The school massacres that have occurred since 1996, however, have reinforced the idea that deadly violence can erupt anywhere, even in a town where the students drive to school in BMWs. According to Joy Turner, who works with young killers in Los Angeles to help them understand what they have done to their victims' families, "What's been real for those of us in the inner city is now real in the suburbs. Violence is like a movie: it's coming to a theater near you."

Ironically, many commentators believe that the relative safety of affluent suburban schools is what makes them vulnerable to a rampage such as the one carried out by Harris and Klebold. Since the staff of inner-city schools have much more experience in dealing with violence, they have learned to spot and defuse potential risks quickly, but the quiet safety of Littleton lulled parents and teachers there into a false sense of security. "It may be hard for so-called safe communities to accept the fact that their children can inflict as much mayhem as, and maybe more than, those from less privileged environments and to take the tough steps that [inner-city] schools like mine have learned are the price of protection," writes Patrick Welsh, an English teacher at T.C. Williams High School in Alexandria, Virginia.

In the wake of the school shootings, social critics have focused on the usual array of suspected causes of juvenile violence: media violence, the availability of guns, lax parenting, and the breakdown of authority. The carnage at Littleton, however, has shed light on another aspect of school life that seldom receives attention—bullying. According to many commentators, bullying is often an underlying cause of school violence. The National School Safety Center calls bullying "the most enduring and underrated problem in American schools." It is widely acknowledged that Eric Harris and Dylan Klebold were favored targets for verbal and physical harassment by Columbine's athletes. Harris and Klebold, along with others of outcast status at Columbine, were regularly slammed into lockers and called "faggots." Luke Woodham, the boy responsible for the shooting in Pearl, Mississippi, was also constantly abused by the popular students at his school, as were many of the other perpetrators of school shootings. Some observers speculate that Harris, Klebold, Woodham, and the others were pushed over the edge by years of torment. Woodham himself wrote a letter explaining the motivation behind his rampage: "I am not insane. I am angry. I killed because people like me are mistreated every day. I did this to show society, 'Push us and we will push back.'"

Bullying is often violent itself, yet most parents and teachers down-

play bullying rather than considering it a serious form of school violence. For example, Bill Head of Marietta, Georgia, thought little of
the bloody noses and taunts his son Brian endured at school. "I
thought it was normal kid stuff," he relates, until the day in 1994
when Brian walked into his classroom, waved a gun around, and then
shot himself in front of his classmates. Many observers feel that violent episodes will continue until educators and parents take a strong
stance against all forms of bullying. David Yarovesky, a student and
self-described social outcast at Calabasas High School in Los Angeles,
hopes that massacres such as Littleton will draw attention to the
often-cruel social hierarchy of school. While he does not condone the
actions of the perpetrators of the school shootings, Yarovesky does
sympathize with ostracized students like them. "I feel that [the
Columbine massacre] had to happen," Yarovesky said. "Someone had
to notice that something was wrong at school."

School Violence: Contemporary Issues Companion examines the effect
that bullying and other types of violence have on students, parents,
and teachers, as well as various other topics concerning violent
behavior in schools. In the chapters that follow, discussions focus on
the causes of school violence, the prevention of violent outbursts by
students, and personal narratives of survivors of violent episodes at
school. These essays provide a comprehensive overview of one of the
most disturbing issues facing American schools today.

CHAPTER 1

THE NATURE OF SCHOOL VIOLENCE

THE CHAOTIC ATMOSPHERE OF SCHOOL

Jeanne Wright

Jeanne Wright, a contributor to the *Washington Post,* examines the breakdown in discipline and the rise in violent behavior in schools, focusing on several public school systems in the Washington, D.C., area. Wright points out that although a relatively small group of disruptive students is responsible for most violent incidents, their presence severely undermines teachers' ability to maintain order in the classroom. The uncooperative nature of many parents and the threat of legal action further impede teachers' efforts to maintain a safe atmosphere in the classroom, Wright explains.

Teachers across the country—from tough inner-city schools to affluent suburban districts—are growing increasingly frustrated and fearful that their classrooms and hallways are being disrupted and turned into battlefields by a few violent and ill-behaved students intent on creating chaos.

Incidents of violence and disorderly conduct—shootings, profanity and plain failure to obey rules—are escalating. On May 14, 1997, science teacher Lawrence C. Hoyer, 60, collapsed and died after breaking up a fight among several girls at Wilde Lake High School in Columbia, Maryland; and a 15-year-old Woodrow Wilson High School student in the District of Columbia was charged on May 13, 1997, with assault for allegedly hitting a teacher in the face.

"We're losing it in our schools," says Richard Williams, an English teacher at Wheaton High School and secretary of the Montgomery County (Maryland) Federation of Teachers. "There is no discipline now. We're letting a few ruin it for the majority of kids who are eager to learn."

On February 7, 1997, Williams, 51, watched as his own classroom became a battlefield when an enraged student stormed in and charged after him, trashing furniture and struggling with other students who came to Williams's rescue. The teenage boy, whom Williams had failed the previous semester, created such havoc, "the classroom resembled a barroom brawl scene," Williams told administrators in his official incident report.

The Chaotic Condition of the Classroom

Wheaton Principal Joseph Dalton says the incident, the first of its kind in the more than 15 years he's been at the school, "was very severe. The student is no longer in the school. Nobody had to worry about that 10 years ago. Unfortunately these are realities now. Those are the kinds of things that scare educators."

Angry over what he says is the intolerable level of bad behavior among students and the lack of enforcement of rules, teacher Michael Reynolds resigned in 1996 from his fifth-grade teaching job at Barnard Elementary School in Washington, D.C.

Reynolds, who had switched careers at the age of 40 to become a teacher, lasted only two full school years in the District.

"I knew I couldn't change the world, but I needed to do something in my life that mattered" for children, says Reynolds. "I wasn't naive about the hard realities of an urban school system. But this was chaos. . . . I wasn't teaching. I was just coping and making sure these kids got through the day alive," says Reynolds, who since has been substitute teaching in Montgomery County. Kids from a crisis intervention class would "come into my classroom and yell obscenities. . . . I had fifth-graders who couldn't read."

Reynolds decided to resign the day a fifth-grader came into his classroom and told the teacher—in front of all of his students—to perform a lewd act on him. "Half of my class was in hysterics" and the rest acted uninterested, says Reynolds. "I was in a rage."

Barnard Principal Erma Jefferson declined to comment on students' behavior at the school, but says, "I'm not sure if it was all kids [problems] or a lack of discipline management on the teacher's part."

According to Barbara Bullock, president of the Washington (D.C.) Teachers Union, "The problem is, they don't have a unified disciplinary plan in D.C. schools. It varies from school to school." For example, she says, fighting in one school may result in a suspension, but in another school, the child would be suspended but be allowed to wander the school halls all day.

Frustration

While teachers and administrators are quick to stress that most children in the schools are good and eager to learn, they're frustrated. Even a disrespectful student who constantly mouths off to teachers can disrupt an entire class.

Many of these discipline problems, observes Sylven Beck, director of the graduate Elementary Education Model Program at George Washington University, reflect the "general unraveling of the social fabric." Family breakups, conflicting value systems and exposure to violence all have a role in children's behavior, say Beck and other educators.

Today's teachers can be in more diverse, multicultural classrooms where not everyone may speak the same language, Beck notes. The classroom also may have children with learning disabilities or emotional difficulties.

"We always preach at the university that what teachers should be doing is to provide a safety net for children coming to school who do not have one at home," says Beck.

Unfortunately, when the bell rings at the end of the school day, "they go back into an environment that undoes everything a teacher tries to do during the day. So you have children who are frustrated and confused living in two worlds with different standards."

And if teachers are in a school setting where they don't have the support of administrators or parents, they are isolated and frustrated.

On that level, the issue of school discipline has become highly politicized, pitting teachers against administrators.

Some teachers blame school officials for failing to enforce rules and back up classroom teachers when they discipline students. They complain that administrators are too reluctant to take action against unruly students for fear of lawsuits by parents. Some critics fault educators for doing everything to improve students' "self-esteem" at the expense of teaching them rules and responsibilities.

Some administrators, on the other hand, accuse teachers and union representatives of exaggerating problems of violence and unruly behavior in the schools.

"My message to them is we are on the same side of this issue," says Dolores Bohen, Fairfax County, Virginia, Public Schools spokeswoman. "We don't tolerate student assaults on teachers either. We want to do something about student discipline, too. But they [some teachers and union leaders] have chosen to do it from an antagonistic perspective by accusing the school system of not wanting to do it and of not supporting teachers."

A Growing Problem

The 900,000-member American Federation of Teachers (AFT) has hit schools hard on the issues of safety of teachers and students.

"We just want the schools to get better and safer," insists Joseph Monte, president of the Montgomery County Federation of Teachers. "It won't work if teachers don't have more authority. We as a teachers' union have to make ways to make sure the teachers are protected . . . because the teacher is also protecting every kid in the classroom."

The statistics prove there's a big problem, says Rick Nelson, president of the Fairfax County Federation of Teachers. During the 1995–96 school year, 327 students were recommended for expulsion from Fairfax County schools, including 120 for assaults, 120 for drugs and 41 for weapons, according to numbers released by the school district.

Nelson says there were 13,900 suspensions—for offenses ranging from possession of drugs to fighting, from theft to possession of a beeper—during the 1994–95 school year, with 65 percent of those involved repeat offenders.

Some of what teachers want, according to the AFT, is better enforcement of school rules; more authority and more support from parents, principals and other administrators to deal immediately with discipline in their classes; stiffer penalties for serious offenses; and use of time-out rooms or alternative settings for disruptive students who need to be removed from the class.

The National Education Association (NEA), with 2 million members, also is concerned about safety and discipline and encourages parents, teachers and school officials to work together to teach kids "who is in control at school; insist that everyone is treated with respect and that nobody is above the consequences of the rules," says Lily Eskelson, NEA executive board member and a teacher in Utah.

"Teachers have to know that they are not left out there hanging all by themselves with some kid that is absolutely out of control . . . and parents and teachers need to be able to count on their school district to provide an alternative situation or facility for kids if it gets so severe that we feel people are in danger," says Eskelson.

In Fairfax County, for example, steps are being taken to seriously address discipline issues, says Bohen. She points to the $1.3 million budgeted in January 1997 to assist schools in creating time-out rooms, staffing Saturday schools or providing variations of local alternative schools for problem students.

A handful of schools in the huge Fairfax district already have begun using time-out rooms—also called alternative learning rooms—for disruptive children. Other schools are considering what options would be best implemented on their campuses.

At Hunters Woods Elementary School for the Arts and Sciences in Reston, Principal Linda Goldberg says use of the time-out rooms has been "very successful" in effectively dealing with disruptive or disrespectful behavior. "Teachers don't send children to the time-out room because they look at them crosswise," says Goldberg. The program is for "children that are so needy [behavior-wise] that we are constantly looking for alternatives for them."

Montgomery County schools have had a good "discipline process that over the years has met the needs of most students and effectively dealt with problems," says Principal Dalton. But in light of changes in society, educators need to consider reevaluating the way discipline is dealt with in the school district, he says.

At Wheaton High School, Dalton says most parents are supportive and cooperative with the staff about discipline issues affecting their children. "They want their kids to behave and do well and get the best grades possible. They don't want them causing trouble, using foul language or skipping school," he says.

Not all teachers see such cooperation. NEA's Eskelson says she has encountered parents who object to their children even being made to write on the blackboard [so] that they will refrain from talking in class. She says she used to make disruptive students "drop and do 20 push- ups." But "I had a mother call and just about rip my head off. How could I embarrass her son by making him the object of ridicule?"

The mother of a second-grader at a district elementary school says when a group of boys in her daughter's class were told they could not participate in a classroom party because of bad behavior, one irate mother undermined the teacher by announcing she would pick her son up early that day and take him to a place where he would have even more fun than those attending the class party.

Threats of legal action also color discipline approaches. "Kids are incredibly astute about their legal rights," says Eskelson.

Hayfield High School teacher Deborah Sanville, who teaches students with learning disabilities, believes "school administrations are fearful of parents." The Fairfax County teacher, who in 1995 pressed charges against a student who had physically threatened her in a hallway, says, "We have empowered parents to such a degree that the administration quakes at the thought of a parent coming in. So to avoid possible conflict, whatever the parent wants goes."

Sanville contends that so much emphasis has been put on promoting students' self-esteem that educators are afraid to discipline or demand good behavior from kids because they'll be accused of hurting their self-esteem. "We're raising a generation of ill-behaved, rude kids . . . but, by God, they feel great.

"The bottom line is our kids are losing out," says Sanville. "Most of the kids in school are good, but there's that segment that is bad, ill-behaved, irresponsible and doesn't belong in public schools. Yet they are running the show."

VIOLENT BEHAVIOR IN SCHOOLS IS DECLINING

Terence Monmaney

Terence Monmaney, citing statistics from a survey published in the *Journal of the American Medical Association,* explains that violent incidents in America's schools are becoming less frequent. However, the author writes that media coverage of violent episodes such as the 1999 shooting at Columbine High School in Littleton, Colorado, have fueled the public's erroneous perception that school violence is out of control. Monmaney is a medical writer for the *Los Angeles Times.*

Amid turbulent national debate over school shootings, government researchers are reporting a largely unheralded decline in high school violence in the 1990s, with many fewer students saying that they carried a weapon or engaged in fights than at the beginning of the decade.

In four biennial surveys of more than 45,000 high school students nationwide between 1991 and 1997, the number of youths who said they carried a weapon to school fell by 28%, the researchers found. The number of students who said they got in a schoolyard fight fell by 9%. And the proportion who carried a gun on or off campus dropped 25%.

Reconciling those positive trends with the more recent mass killings on school campuses is difficult, the researchers and other analysts say. But the study, made public in the August 4, 1999, edition of the *Journal of the American Medical Association,* suggests that various efforts to reduce schoolyard dangers have been effective despite the rare outbreak of inexplicable mayhem.

Real Progress

"This is real progress," said study coauthor Thomas Simon, a behavioral scientist at the U.S. Centers for Disease Control and Prevention. . . .

Regarding the school violence study, Simon said it is unclear how students' feelings and behavior might be affected in the long run by recent tragedies such as the fatal shooting of twelve students and a teacher in Littleton, Colorado, in April 1999. But because the study

Excerpted from "High School Violence in Decline," by Terence Monmaney, *Los Angeles Times,* August 4, 1999. Reprinted with permission from the *Los Angeles Times.*

draws on such a large number of students, it "is more representative of what is really happening with kids today," he said.

In Los Angeles County, students have experienced a comparable decline in hostilities and the potential for violence, according to school district data. The 0.06% of students in all grades who were caught with weapons in 1997–98 was nearly one-third the level of the 1990–91 school year. And documented battery has fallen by 30% over the same period.

The trends described in the national study "are consistent with some of the encouraging things we've seen in the schools themselves and among the students," said Wesley Mitchell, chief of the Los Angeles School Police Department.

At the same time, the study conveys an image of high school life in America today that is far from serene, recent improvements notwithstanding. In 1997, 36.6% of youths surveyed said they were in a physical fight, about 15% said they were in a fight on campus, and 8.5% said they had carried a weapon to class in the previous thirty days.

Also, progress was not uniform in all groups surveyed. Defying some of the trends were Latino students, who were somewhat more likely to report being threatened with a weapon or getting in a fight on school property in 1997 compared to 1993, the researchers found. A possible reason for that ethnic disparity, one of the researchers speculated, was that past violence prevention programs may not have sufficiently reflected Latino culture.

Finally, there was no significant drop in the number of students who reported being afraid to go to school, which held at about 4%. Students' perceptions of their safety may be out of line with reality, perhaps because of news media saturation coverage of isolated incidents, scholars said.

The Debate over School Safety

The challenge for parents, students and policymakers is deciding which version of school life is more accurate: the downward trends in violence found by the Centers for Disease Control researchers and others, or the harrowing news videos of frightened students running for their lives at a few now infamous high schools.

The debate over school safety has heated up after the fatal shootings of twenty-two students and teachers at five campuses since March 1998. A *Los Angeles Times* telephone poll of 1,602 Californians in June 1999, found that about 50% of respondents said state schools were unsafe, and 10% of parents with school-age children said their youngsters had been victimized by campus violence.

Barry Glassner, a USC sociology professor and author of *The Culture of Fear,* said the school violence trends parallel those of U.S. society. "While crime rates have been declining for years now," he said, "the fear of crime remains high and the disparity between perception and the actual statistics is striking."

The Centers for Disease Control study drew on surveys of students in public and private high schools in urban, suburban and rural areas. It was part of a larger ongoing project known as the Youth Risk Behavior Surveys, which presents high school students with a ninety-item questionnaire on safety, sexual issues, tobacco and alcohol use and other matters. Some questions about weapons did not appear on the questionnaire until 1993.

In the study, the researchers found that fighting among students went down the greatest among girls, from 34% in 1991 to 26% in 1997.

Between 1993 and 1997, one of the biggest drops was in the proportion of students who said they had carried a weapon to school in the previous month, to 8.5% of those surveyed. Significantly, though, most of that decline was in gun carrying, while carrying other weapons to school did not decline significantly.

Chief Mitchell of the Los Angeles public school police said that conformed with department data showing that some students have switched from guns to knives.

On the whole, he credited a variety of measures for reducing actual and potential violence on campuses, from metal detectors at schools to programs for teaching students nonviolent ways to reduce conflicts to a growing economy.

In Ventura County, California, officials detected slightly more students carrying weapons in 1997–98 than in the previous school year— a rise from eight to ten weapons possessions per 10,000 students.

Simon, of the Centers for Disease Control, said some of the nationwide reductions in violence and the potential for violence appear to reflect initiatives put in place in the early 1990s. "It's possible we're reaping the benefits of those efforts now," he said. "But there's a lot more to do because the level of violence in schools is still unacceptably high."

Researchers acknowledge that some respondents may give false answers in such surveys, but Simon said that they checked the validity of answers by retesting some of the students. In addition, he said, there is little incentive to cheat because the survey was anonymous.

SCHOOL VIOLENCE IS EXAGGERATED BY THE MEDIA

Mike Males

In the following selection, Mike Males, author of *Framing Youth: Ten Myths About the Next Generation,* argues that the media have used the 1999 massacre at Columbine High School in Littleton, Colorado, as an excuse to paint an inaccurately bleak picture of today's teenagers and their school environments. School shootings are actually a rarity, Males writes, and schools are very safe environments for kids. Contrary to popular portrayals, the 1990s have witnessed a decline in violent behavior by teens, he explains. Nevertheless, according to Males, the media persists in portraying teenagers negatively while downplaying the rise in violent behavior among adults.

Littleton, Colorado's school massacre by two Hitler-enamored students [Eric Harris and Dylan Klebold shot and killed 12 classmates and one teacher at Columbine High School on April 20, 1999] gave politicians and the mainstream media an excuse to indulge in their worst anti-youth frenzy yet. Reporters (who did not blame mass-killers such as Timothy McVeigh [who bombed the Alfred P. Murrah Building in Oklahoma City] or Ted Kaczynski [the Unabomber] on "white adult culture") swept into Littleton, sworn to uphold the myth that school shootings were caused by "youth culture": teenage alienation, violent video games and movies, mean-teen cliques, Internet corruptions, and dark adolescent subcultures invading nice (read: suburban) homes to defy the healthy values of nice (read: affluent) parents.

The image of shattered suburban innocence was trumpeted—even though suburbs are no strangers to murder. In Southern California alone, a dozen rampages between 1997 and 1999 by middle-aged, suburban adults armed with high-powered rifles, semi-automatic pistols and assault weapons left a total of 40 dead, including 16 kids—far more than have been killed in the region's schools in decades. Yet politicians, authorities and the news media did not string these slaughters together to warn of "violent midlife culture," backed by scary statistics

Excerpted from "The Monsters on Page One," by Mike Males, *Extra!* July/August 1999. Reprinted with permission from *Extra!*

on the killings of 2,000 to 3,000 children and youths in their homes every year (U.S. Advisory Board on Child Abuse and Neglect, 1995).

The Media's Script

Rather, the media's Littleton script was shaped by politicians—led by President Clinton, who blamed the Littleton shootings on youths corrupted by "the blizzard of popular communications that often undermine" parents' values. From that boilerplate formula, circumstantial details were added, numbingly conformist news stories filed, and thin plots were played and rerun.

Through media-chosen experts and cultural arbiters, established society relentlessly congratulated its good values, culpable only in the failure to monitor and suppress "The Monsters Next Door," as *Time* dubbed the new suburban menace. *Newsweek*'s pure-paranoid issue of May 10, 1999, depicted suburban adolescents as terrifying ciphers: "The secret life of teens," "Their dark romance with risk," "When teens fall apart," "How well do you know your kid?" etc.

Kids are richer, freer and enjoy more opportunity than ever, yet "in survey after survey, many kids—even those on the honor roll—say they feel increasingly alone and alienated, unable to connect with their parents or teachers," diagnosed *Newsweek*'s Barbara Kantrowitz, whose reporting seems to consist of cataloguing stereotypes. She conjured up the genesis of massacre: parent-unsupervised teens in their own world "defined by computer games, TV and movies, where brutality is so common as to be mundane."

"Why Are So Many Teens Alienated?" *U.S. News & World Report* headlined on May 2, 1999, never bothering to prove that many are. *Time*'s May 17, 1999, cover reran a child's face lit in dark Internet glow and the banner "Today's kids grow up in a world of computers and video games."

Pop Culture and Guns

Blaming cultural demons was vicious on the right. ("Goth control," not "gun control," GOP strategist Mike Murphy urged.) Liberals joined in. "There was almost no difference between Republicans and Democrats," Massachusetts Institute of Technology media studies professor Henry Jenkins declared, shaken by the fury at "popular culture" he encountered in Congressional hearings.

On the liberal side, saving "precious children" from "guns" was the agenda—so long as no one important was inconvenienced. "It is criminal how easy it is for children in America to obtain guns," President Clinton declared, straddling all camps. "Every day in America, we lose 13 precious children to gun-related violence." The true number is eight, and Clinton and gun control advocates failed to mention that most are killed by adults. Handgun Control, Inc. called for yet another law against "juvenile possession" of guns to make "this country safer for children without placing undue inconvenience on hunters and law-abiding citizens." Or on the 40ish suburban men whose shooting sprees left more kids dead in California in a few months than school killings had in a decade.

And, while it's hard to argue with the press and psychological lobbies' oft-repeated panacea, more school counselors are a dubious way to deter shootings. Littleton was one of the few cities in the nation with a juvenile assessment center, and at least two gunboys had been under psychiatric care (medicated, in fact) before their rampages.

The Truth About Teens

Amid the agenda-hawking, no one had any use for optimistic facts about youth that rained on cultural warriors' parades. A major spoiler: In the last 20 years, and especially in the last decade, as guns, violent games and media, and other cultural ills proliferated, murder, rape, other serious crime, petty crime, violent death, traffic crashes, suicidal deaths, drug abuse, gun fatality and just about every other malaise declined among those supposedly most corrupted by pop culture— white, suburban, middle- and upper-class teens.

Another spoiler for culture warriors itching to crusade: Poll after poll of teens show that an astounding 90 percent view themselves as healthy and self-confident, four-fifths get along well with their parents (would that the parents got along so well with each other), and four-fifths have trusting relationships with other adults. When asked about major influences on their lives, parents, religion and teachers topped teens' lists. The National Association of Secretaries of State survey, conducted in February 1999, found volunteer work among today's teenagers, especially for services "such as soup kitchens, hospitals and schools" that "help others in a personal way" has risen sharply to "record high levels."

It would be hard to imagine a younger generation less messed-up and alienated than today's. In a rare analytical post-Littleton article, Sheryl Stolberg reported in the May 8, 1999, edition of the [*New York Times*] that school shootings "are so rare" that the Littleton massacre "was the statistical equivalent of a needle in a haystack." Dr. Jim Mercy, the Centers for Disease Control's violence prevention scientist, told Stolberg: "The reality is that schools are very safe environments for our kids."

Masking the Truth

Why, then, are just about every authority and reporter bombarding an apparently receptive public with Suburban Teen Armageddon? Perhaps because teenagers aren't the hostile ones; adults are. Public Agenda's June 1997 poll found that while 70 percent to 80 percent of teens expressed favorable views of adults, two-thirds of adults expressed blanket negative views of adolescents.

The unsettling nature of the real "dark side" the media and politicians refuse to engage is that middle-class and affluent adult behaviors have drastically deteriorated in recent decades. Since 1980, hard-drug and alcohol overdose deaths and hospital emergency treatments have tripled, and felony arrest and imprisonment rates have doubled, among adults in the 30–50 age range, particularly whites. Family violence, bitter spousal warfare and divorce, and personal disarray are gripping middle-aged whites as never before.

The growing rage at young people fueled by mainstream media and authorities increasingly takes on the character of witch-hunt hysteria. "We have been unwilling participants in the events of the past few days," said a large gothic website's "Statement Against Violence Everywhere" in April 1999. "The dark imagery we use to express ourselves has come under close scrutiny in the media. . . . We have been threatened, cajoled, and questioned by the world."

As with the creation of the black or brown "teenage superpredator" to mask devastating job loss, poverty and institutional racism in inner cities, the media's new suburban gothic, killer-geek image masks worsening white adult behavior. The irony is that young people's media-lambasted alternative families—the goths, raves, zines, posses, Internet groupings—may be one reason why youths are not aping the deterioration of adults around them.

Manufacturing Fear

Like the media everywhere, papers in Orange County, California, declared that guns infest local schools and Littleton–style school carnage "could happen here." They didn't quote anyone who had actually seen a gun in a school, and didn't mention that there had been no murder or shooting in an Orange County school in anyone's memory—an amazing safety record in a county of 2.9 million where police respond to gun violence in a home every third day, and 6,000 people have been killed or hurt by gunfire in the last decade in just about every place except a school.

Yet, two weeks after Littleton, suburban Orange County suffered its first school murders, perhaps the most bafflingly tragic ones anywhere. A 39-year-old man, declaring his intent to "execute . . . innocent" children to avenge his girlfriend's rejection, deliberately gunned his Cadillac into a Costa Mesa preschool yard, crushing a three- and a four-year-old to death, leaving two small children in critical condition, and injuring three more.

Outside of California, few heard about this school tragedy. No national cameras, no blaring headlines. ABC did not run the story; CNN and Associated Press carried only minor briefs. No mention of Costa Mesa's grisly school murders at the White House conference on school violence. School slaughter by a middle-ager wielding a Cadillac didn't fit the media's or politicians' needs, thank you.

School Bullies

Patrick J. Kiger

According to Patrick J. Kiger, a freelance writer based in Washington, D.C., most of the public is unaware of the rampant occurrence of violent bullying in many schools. Kiger writes that some children are terrorized to such a degree that they suffer serious physical injuries, while other children commit suicide to escape the torment inflicted on them by bullies. School officials are often to blame for the prevalence of bullying, Kiger explains, ~~ because they frequently look the other way when bullies physically accost other students, rather than taking strong measures to stop the violence.

It was 3:30 on a Thursday afternoon in November 1996 when 13-year-old Andy (name has been changed) walked out the door of Crittenden Middle School in Mountain View, California, having stayed after classes for a tutoring session. The school is in a neighborhood of modest ranch houses, their lawns strewn with toys—the sort of place where parents feel comfortable letting their children play outside unattended. On his way home, Andy didn't have to fear gang shootings or drug dealers battling for turf. Yet the eighth grader had a different menace to worry about.

As Andy left school for the day, he found himself surrounded by five adolescent boys. The leader of the pack, a 14-year-old high school freshman named Jared, stood close to six feet tall and weighed 240 pounds, nearly twice as much as Andy. Jared grabbed Andy and held him so the other boys could punch him. Then Jared warned that if Andy didn't come with them willingly, if they had to make him, things were going to get worse.

Andy knew to take the threat seriously; this was not his first encounter with Jared and company. Only a couple of weeks earlier, they had roughed up Andy at a party, then repeatedly held him underwater in a swimming pool—just for laughs. Too intimidated to tattle, and too fearful of retribution, Andy didn't say a word to his family about the harrowing encounter.

Ask most parents to conjure up a schoolyard bully and they'll remember the big kid who took other children's lunch money or

Excerpted from "Kids Who Terrorize Kids," by Patrick J. Kiger, *Good Housekeeping*, October 1998. Reprinted with permission from the author.

shoved them around when the teacher wasn't looking—an endurable if unpleasant part of growing up. But they'd scarcely picture a living nightmare like Jared, whose sadistic acts against fellow students ran to dangerous extremes.

On this particular afternoon, Jared had plotted some really twisted fun. He and his buddies marched Andy to the mobile home where Jared lived with his mother, who at this time of day was still at the computer company where she worked. Along the way, they smacked their prey over the head with his loose-leaf binder. Once inside, one boy hastily cleared the furniture from the living room while the others handcuffed Andy. Jared started throwing punches, then all the boys joined in, using their fists and feet.

Over the next two hours, Andy, pleading for mercy all the while, was whipped with a chain, burned with candle wax, and shot in the back with a BB gun. With dusk approaching, a battered, bruised, and bleeding Andy was tossed out the door with a warning: Don't tell anyone what happened to you.

After staggering to a fast-food restaurant, Andy telephoned his father with a trumped-up tale of having been kidnapped and brutalized by a band of men. Enter the police, who finally persuaded Andy to tell the truth. Jared and his cohorts were promptly arrested and charged with kidnapping, assault, and torture.

The Prevalence of Bullying

If Jared were an isolated example, we could all rest easier. But the bully problem is bigger than most of us think. Seventeen percent of junior high school students admit to being victims of in-school intimidation, physical assault, or robbery, according to a 1995 survey conducted by the National Center for Education Statistics. And authorities who've investigated bullying suspect that the numbers are much higher. "Thirty to forty-five percent of kids in the suburbs I'm familiar with tell us they're being bullied," says Leawood, Kansas, police officer Randy Wiler, who's trained teachers and administrators at schools throughout the Kansas City, Kansas, area on how to deal with the problem.

What's more, today's bully is not just an inner-city phenomenon. Nine percent of suburban students reported being victims of violence, roughly the same proportion as in urban schools, according to a 1997 study by the Reason Public Policy Institute, a Los Angeles–based think tank. The trend is escalating; fifty-four percent of principals of suburban schools polled during 1988 to 1993 said violence had increased on their school premises. Not only is the frequency of incidents up, but so is the level of ferocity. For example, in suburban Fresno, California, in February 1996, a high school junior was surrounded by a dozen other boys outside the lunchroom and beaten so severely that he suffered a concussion and temporary memory loss. One attacker subsequently was convicted of felony assault. Researchers at Tulane University in New Orleans found that eight percent of suburban high school students thought it was okay to shoot someone who had offended or insulted them, and twenty percent thought it was appropriate to open fire if someone stole from them.

Indeed, in the most extreme cases, bullies do graduate to killing. Witness the shooting deaths of four girls and a teacher outside a middle school in Jonesboro, Arkansas, in March 1997, allegedly by two boys, 11 and 13 years old. [Mitchell Johnson and Andrew Golden were convicted of murder in August 1998.] The 13-year-old, Mitchell Johnson, was described by one schoolmate as a bully who "could pick on anybody that would let him." Just two months later, in Springfield, Oregon, 15-year-old Kip Kinkel, who had "an anger problem," according to one classmate, allegedly shot his parents to death, after which, armed with a semiautomatic rifle and a backpack full of ammunition, he went to school and allegedly opened fire on his classmates, killing two and wounding twenty-two.

How Children Turn Cruel

Jared's troubles surfaced early on. School records describe him as having "control problems" and being "defiant and belligerent" as far back as second grade. He was fanatical about the World Wrestling Federation and loved to act out the violent fantasies he spent countless hours watching on TV. Jared's mother, divorced from his father, attributes Jared's troubles to a learning disability and severe attention deficit disorder. After the boy's arrest, the California Youth Authority mental-health team assigned to his case said Jared had a propensity for dangerous behavior and was "an immature, intensely self-centered, and probably truly narcissistic individual who sees his own behavior as acceptable in every case."

Jared's mother had a close, protective relationship with her son—and that, authorities argue, may have only contributed to the problem. The mental-health team theorized that "Jared's mother has condoned and excused her son's negative behaviors for many years, not holding him responsible and thereby exacerbating such behaviors. Both Jared and his mother believe that he is misunderstood and mistreated and is just fine the way he is." Indeed, despite Jared's eventual guilty plea to kidnapping, attempted torture, and "using force likely to cause great bodily harm," his mother claims he was actually the victim—of teasing by peers about his size and weight. One day four years ago, his mother says, "Jared came home and stood in front of our full-length mirror and said, 'Mommy, am I scary?' And I told him, 'No, honey, you're not scary, you're just a big handsome boy.'" (In a chilling footnote, after Jared's arrest, his mother was arrested for allegedly ramming her truck into a car driven by the mother of a witness in the case against her son. She eventually pled no contest to felony hit-and-run and was sentenced to 200 days in jail and five years of probation. She also had to pay $1,600 in restitution to the victim.)

The consequences of coddling bullies can be tragic. In April 1998, a 12-year-old Wayne, New Jersey, boy brought a pellet gun to school, hoping to scare a bully into leaving him alone; he ended up suspended from school, then pled guilty to unlawfully possessing a weapon. And in 1993, after several years of torment from bullies who'd bang his head into lockers and trip him in hallways, 14-year-old Curtis Taylor of Burlington, Iowa, killed himself.

When Schools Pass the Buck

Clearly, kids can't be expected to solve a bullying problem by themselves. The trouble is, parents can't count on schools to protect their children, either. Victims often charge that authorities don't do enough to prevent bullying and sometimes even look the other way. For example, Jared's school records describe him as difficult, according to law-enforcement officials who've reviewed them, but the files contain no mention of attacks, and the principals at both middle schools he attended say they don't recall any seriously violent incidents.

All of which leads Rick Gardner, the Santa Clara County deputy district attorney who prosecuted Jared in juvenile court, to take a skeptical view. "When you've got a kid with this many problems, it's hard to believe that the schools didn't notice his violent behavior," he says. And the parents of another of Jared's victims recall that shortly after they went to the school to demand protection, Jared was abruptly transferred; the principal contended that she discovered by chance that Jared actually lived within the boundary of a neighboring school district.

In fact, schools have been found to neglect documenting bullies' attacks and to pass the problem along to someone else, according to the National School Safety Center's Ronald Stephens, himself a former school administrator. "A lot of administrators don't want a paper trail," he explains. "It's fear of litigation and a reluctance to look bad."

Desperate parents have resorted to legal action. In Export, Pennsylvania, Elizabeth Barcellino recalls the day in the fall of 1996 when her daughter, Christina, then a seventh grader at Franklin Regional Junior High School, came home from school terrified because two girls on the bus had tried to set her hair on fire. After Barcellino reported the attack to a school official, the situation worsened, according to a lawsuit filed by the Barcellinos and another family, the Clingers, whose daughter was also harassed. The bullies and their friends began harassing Christina and her classmate, Jessica Clinger, staring at them menacingly and hitting and shoving them in school hallways.

Instead of taking action to stop the bullies, the lawsuit alleges, the school's vice principal advised the girls to keep a low profile and wait for the bullies to move on to someone else. At another point, he sent the two girls home, fearing he could not guarantee their safety. Eventually the school board assigned a teacher's aide to escort Christina and Jessica to classes, but the bullies allegedly remained undaunted; they continued to harass the pair in the hallways even in the escort's presence. Eventually, the parents of the victimized girls withdrew them from the school. (A lawyer representing the school district argued in court that a school does not have a legal duty to protect students from other students.)

Like the Barcellinos and the Clingers, parents in other states have tried to pressure schools to take action by going to court. In Brooksville, Florida, Al Holm was aghast when his daughter, then 12, came home from school in October 1996 holding an icepack to her head because she'd been punched by a bully on the school bus. When the school failed to punish her attacker, Holm enrolled his daughter in a private school and filed a suit against the school district. Though the school suit is ongoing, the bully pled no contest to battery and was sentenced to community service.

Stopping Bullies in Their Tracks

Some parents, through trial and error, have found ways to work successfully with schools. Lydia Brown of Mansfield, Texas, says that when her son, now 13, first told her he was being harassed by school bullies in 1996, she didn't grasp the severity of the situation. Instead, she did as many parents would: told her son to either fight back or ignore his tormentors. One day in March 1997, after being chased home and pelted with rocks as he frantically tried to unlock the door, the normally nonviolent boy grabbed his BB gun and began shooting at the bullies in frustration. Later, he confided to his mother that he'd considered suicide as an escape.

Brown had five meetings with school officials but says that as far as she could tell little was done that made much difference. Citing school records' confidentiality, officials wouldn't even tell her if the bullies had been disciplined.

When her son moved on to junior high, Brown asked for a meeting with her son's new principal and teachers. "I gave them a list of the bullies from the last school," she recalls. "I told them, 'If he has a problem with these kids, you know this is part of a pattern, not just an isolated thing.'" The school's principal, she says, let the bullies know that they were being watched to make sure they didn't pick on anyone in the future. At the start of the school year, there was a minor incident; the principal promptly suspended the bullies for five days, and there have been no further problems.

Meanwhile, in California, Jared's case was well out of the hands of school officials. A juvenile-court judge, citing Jared's "horrendous conduct and misbehavior," sentenced him to a state youth authority prison. (His companions were variously sentenced to reform schools and a local facility for juvenile offenders.) "I hope, for the sake of his victims, [Jared] stays in prison for as long as possible," the mother of one of his victims testified at the hearing.

She won't get her wish. Prosecutor Gardner says that as a juvenile, Jared is likely to serve no more than four years behind bars—and possibly less. Gardner hopes the shock of incarceration will keep Jared from becoming one of the estimated sixty percent of childhood bullies who go on to commit adult crimes. But the prosecutor isn't optimistic: "Anybody who doesn't have any empathy and tends to get enjoyment out of hurting other people—that sort of young person can grow up to become one of your Charles Mansons, your Jeffrey Dahmers. They always present a risk."

VIOLENCE IN AN INNER-CITY SCHOOL

Mark Stricherz

In the following article, Mark Stricherz, a reporter for *New Repub-lic* magazine, examines the dangerous conditions at the inner-city Northern High School in Baltimore, Maryland. Despite a school security force of fifteen officers, the author reports, shoot-ings, assaults, rapes, and vandalism plague Northern. According to Stricherz, the problems at Northern are a reflection of the nightmarish conditions—drug addiction, broken families, vio-lent crime—found in this inner-city neighborhood where the school's star athlete and 1997 class valedictorian were both shot and killed.

It's not every day that a high school makes national news, but then it's not every day a principal suspends nearly two-thirds of the stu-dent body—which is what happened in November 1997, at Balti-more's Northern High School. When principal Alice Morgan Brown announced over the public address system that students should pick up their report cards after school, 1,200 students disobeyed, and she decided to suspend all of them. It was, some said, the largest suspen-sion in the history of American education.

In the media frenzy that ensued, some hailed Brown for her gutsy attempt to impose order, while others called for her dismissal. Within days, everyone from National Public Radio to CNN had dispatched correspondents; Brown even appeared on the *Today* show. And, for a week or two, education experts emerged to explain why the crisis at Northern was an argument in favor of this or that pet school-reform idea. But all of the hand-wringing over the suspensions obscured the real story. Whatever Brown's culpability, the roots of Northern's crisis lie not on school grounds but in the ghetto where most Northern stu-dents live—and where the problems are so profound as to be beyond the reach of local and even state government.

To get to the cafeteria at Northern, you have to pass through the school's lone main entrance—the place where Brown, on the day of the suspensions, dramatically (if temporarily) barred the doors to an estimated 1,000 students, many of whom refused her order to go to their homerooms while chanting, "Hell, no, we won't go!" Then you walk through long, windowless corridors and pass about 30 lockers that appear to have been blown up by cherry bombs. In front of the cafeteria, off to the left, there's a wide black grate that prevents students from roaming the halls. Inside, eight of the cafeteria's 30 benches are broken, their legs crumpled. Red soft drink is splattered across the room.

According to police, the cafeteria played a role in the murder of 15-year-old Wayne Martin Rabb Jr. On January 9, 1998, Rabb apparently got into an argument over, literally, spilled milk; after school, three teens allegedly beat him with a baseball bat so severely that he needed an ambulance. A month later, Rabb was shot twice outside a video store, allegedly by a 16-year-old who had attended Northern.

"A Kafkaesque Nightmare"

Such behavior is pretty much the norm at ghetto schools. In 1993, 23 percent of urban school districts reported drive-by shootings at school. Even by these standards, though, Northern—a 20-acre campus set in a mostly blue-collar part of northeastern Baltimore—is in serious trouble. Longtime *Baltimore Sun* education writer Mike Bowler says the school has become "a Kafkaesque nightmare," and, except for a few fine academic programs, he's probably right. The 1997–1998 school year opened with the rape of a 14-year-old girl in a bathroom, and it ended as an off-campus thug shot at a school cop. (All this despite a force of up to 15 school security guards.) Seventy-seven percent of students are "chronically absent"—they miss over 20 school days a year.

In general, Northern's teachers express deep frustration. In November 1997, Mary Robinson quit after one student threatened in class to kill her, she says. "He said, 'I will be back for you, and I will be back to drop you,'" Robinson recalls. At least three teachers in 1997 were assaulted. "We may have one or two schools that have similar problems, but the problems at Northern are extreme, unusual," says Marcia Brown, former president of the city's teachers union.

School insiders blame Principal Brown, a former professor at Morgan State University who had never been a principal before. "You know what happened," chortles French teacher Stanley Naj, "when El Nino dropped unexpectedly on Florida?" Brown's critics have a point. For the first few weeks of school, hundreds of students lacked schedules, and teachers lacked class lists. "It was total chaos," says one teacher. "It took weeks to correct." And never did school officials return a phone call Wayne Rabb's parents had made after their son told them he felt unsafe at school—a call urging that their son be transferred. (Brown declined to be interviewed for this story.)

Broken Families and Bad Peer Groups

But in many ways the problems at Northern are not really problems with Northern. They have more to do with problems the famous

Coleman report on blacks and education identified back in 1966: bad parents and peer groups. "When coke hit Baltimore in the 1980s," Edward Burns and David Simon write in *The Corner: A Year in the Life of an Inner-City Neighborhood*, "it went beyond the existing addict population, gathering a new market share, for the first time bringing the women to the corner in startling numbers." This introduced a new dynamic: Because women too were using cocaine, the drug's subculture, combined with all the other familiar inner-city blights, exerted tremendous sway over children.

In a way even jaded observers would find disturbing, Northern's students have suffered. For instance, their lives at home are wholly foreign to their lives in class. "They can tear up a school," Burns, a teacher at a middle school which serves Northern, says of what he calls "corner" mentality kids. "The logic of the corner does not apply in classrooms, and unfortunately these kids become very frustrated and don't do well." As if the prevalence of broken families was not bad enough, now there is a new phenomenon: families without parents. Robinson says as many as two-thirds of Northern's students either have no parents, have their own kids, or are raising siblings.

Even the student elite grow up in shockingly bad environments. In late September 1997, Northern paid tribute to the school's starting quarterback and the previous year's valedictorian, both of whom were shot and killed not far from their homes: the quarterback, Rocco Cash, was killed in a drive-by shooting, and the valedictorian, Maishan St. Patrick Nelson, was, according to police, shot by a teenager when he made a wrong turn into a drug-infested neighborhood.

Still, Northern is not doomed, or at least it doesn't have to be. Brown will probably be fired, and that will help, school officials say; if a good principal signs on, the school could become less violent and chaotic. But reformers will have to think in grander terms. (Which is saying something: The city's schools were overhauled in 1997.) They could look to the federal government, but Washington provides only seven percent of school funding. Vouchers are no panacea. Even President Clinton's school reforms would barely affect Northern. The proposal to shrink class sizes, for example, only applies to grades one through three. But loftier schemes are not on the table; nobody is talking about Northern anymore.

SCHOOL MASSACRES ARE ON THE RISE IN THE SUBURBS

Barbara A. Serrano

Though overall school violence is declining in America, mass shootings in suburban and rural areas are becoming more common, explains *Seattle Times* staff writer Barbara A. Serrano in the following selection. Serrano points out that suburban schools, though they are still generally safer than inner-city schools, are experiencing a rise in deadly incidents partly because suburban teachers and students are not as prepared as their urban counterparts when it comes to dealing with violence. Urban school officials and students have had much more experience with violent behavior, and as a result, they are more mindful of the risks on their campuses and are better able to prevent a violent incident, Serrano writes.

Deadly violence is still rare in U.S. schools and has been getting rarer since 1992. Still, researchers are taking a hard look at the tragedies in Littleton, Colorado, and elsewhere in an effort to identify the causes.

A disgruntled student smuggles a high-powered weapon on to a high school campus and goes on a shooting spree, leaving dead bodies and bloody carnage behind. It happened in Moses Lake, Washington, West Paducah, Kentucky, Jonesboro, Arkansas, Springfield, Oregon, and Littleton, Colorado—all in rural and suburban schools.

Still, parents living in the affluent Denver suburb of Littleton are having a tough time comprehending the April 1999 massacre by Columbine High School students Dylan Klebold and Eric Harris.

Why Here?

How could something so irrational happen here, some ask, instead of in big cities like, say, Los Angeles and Detroit?

Researchers are wondering the same thing. In contrast to the gang- and drug-related killings that wracked urban neighborhoods in the 1980s and early 1990s, the recent phenomenon of multiple-victim school shootings is so suburban and rural in character that researchers and educators are beginning to study it as a new form of violence.

Excerpted from "How Can We Know Our Schools are Safe? The Numbers Tell the Story," by Barbara Serrano, *The Seattle Times*, May 2, 1999. Reprinted with permission from the author and *The Seattle Times*.

"It's happening in places that we didn't think it would," said Daniel Flannery, director of the Institute for the Study and Prevention of Violence at Kent State University in Ohio. "That's what people have to begin to understand. It only takes one or two troubled kids to do something like this, so nobody's immune."

Klebold, 17, and Harris, 18, introduced terrorist tactics into the spate of recent assaults when they sneaked homemade bombs—more than 50 at last count—onto the Columbine High School campus and hurled explosives at their victims. They killed 12 students and a teacher before killing themselves.

It was the nation's 11th multiple-death shooting incident at a school since 1996.

But while television images of paramedics and SWAT teams rushing onto schoolyards have been seared into the national conscience, deadly violence is still a rarity on American campuses and has been on the decline since 1992. And suburban and rural schools remain safer environments for children than their inner-city counterparts.

A *Seattle Times* review of national statistics compiled by the National School Safety Center in Southern California shows that the number of violent-death incidents in both urban and suburban neighborhoods has dropped dramatically since 1992.

But school shootings that result in numerous deaths are becoming more common and more lethal.

No one professes to know why. In and of themselves, multiple-death shootings are so new that no one has conducted the research to determine whether the trend means anything, or is simply a statistical fluke. But plenty of theories are starting to circulate.

Cities Ready for Violence

Some point out that urban school districts have been in the business of violence prevention longer, and perhaps are more sophisticated and mindful of the potential risks lurking on campuses. Inner-city schools, forced to grapple with gang problems and the crack-cocaine epidemic in the 1980s, were the first in the country to institute metal detectors, anger-management programs and armed security officers.

An inner-city kid would more likely get caught trying to sneak ammunition onto campuses that have had security officers, surveillance cameras and other precautionary measures in place for years, and so would be less likely to try.

But maybe, others say, it has deeper cultural roots. The rampages unleashed by young gunmen like Harris and Klebold have had an eerie make-believe feel to them, as though they were acting out some practiced role in a movie.

For many inner-city children, on the other hand, deadly violence is no Hollywood adventure or video game but part of everyday life, says Henry Duvall, spokesman for the Council of the Great City Schools, a

Washington, D.C.–based organization that represents the country's largest 54 school districts.

He subscribes to the notion that urban students are more apt to want to protect their campuses, not turn them into killing fields. "Quite frankly, in some of the inner cities, the schools are really safe havens," Duvall said. "It's safer in the schools than it is at home," where children may confront abuse of one form or another.

"For some of these kids," he added, "it's more dangerous for them just to be walking the streets."

Even when shooting deaths in the cities peaked in the early 1990s, they usually involved a single victim or were aimed at rival gang members.

The shooting rampages in suburban and rural campuses, by contrast, have been more random and, in some instances, resembled suicide missions. Not one of the deadly mass shootings has occurred in an inner-city area, and nearly all of the victims have been white.

A Social Epidemic

James Garbarino, a Cornell University professor and author of a book called *Lost Boys: Why Our Sons Turn Violent and How We Can Save Them,* views the shooting assaults as a social epidemic that is evolving and mutating as it progresses from cities into small towns and suburban neighborhoods.

He suggests that part of the reason inner-city, minority youth have not been involved in multiple-death shootings on school campuses is because they don't identify with school in the same way white, middle-class young men do.

The most troubled city teens have already "checked out" physically or mentally from school or are serving time in detention centers by ages of 16 or 17, so they wouldn't necessarily act out their aggressions on campus, Garbarino said.

"School is not the central focus of their lives," he said. "Whereas for these middle-class kids, even when they have difficult lives, they are shielded and supported and carried through their early years. When they get to be teenagers, their troubles crystallize. And school is the place where their psychological lives take place. They rise and fall there."

Despite the media's attention on real and threatened firearm assaults and bombings, crime in public schools has actually gone down—not up.

A 1998 report by the U.S. Departments of Justice and Education says children have more chance of getting killed by lightning than suffering a violent death on campus, less than one chance in a million. Only one in ten schools surveyed by the government reported any serious violent crimes.

Overall, the number of violent school-related deaths has dropped from a peak of 53 in the 1992–1993 school year to 24 so far in the 1998–1999 year. Without the shootings at Columbine, the number would be at an all-time low this decade—nine.

And it's still urban and minority students who are most at risk.

Researchers at the Centers for Disease Control and Prevention (CDC) in Atlanta have conducted the only comprehensive review of violent school-related deaths, and they say the rate of urban students being killed on or near campus is nine times higher than the rate in small towns and rural communities.

Laura Ross-Greiner, a consultant at the Center for the Study and Prevention of Violence at the University of Colorado, says: "I don't know that this is a fluke. It just happens that all of these kids are feeling alienated or isolated. It could just as easily happen to kids in city areas."

The steady string of multiple-death shootings from 1996 to 1999, nonetheless, has caused researchers there to give the incidents their own classification.

They are updating the CDC's 1994 study on violent school deaths and zeroing in on the trend of school shootings in suburbs and small towns.

Tom Simon, a behavioral scientist at the CDC, says he and his colleagues may not be able to pinpoint underlying causes but, at the very least, will highlight any characteristics that make urban, suburban and rural shootings different from one another.

Researchers are particularly intrigued by the wave of mass shootings since their occurrence now averages five per year.

"It's unclear whether people will have an answer to why it's happening," Simon said. "It's safer to say we'll be able to describe the incidents in more detail."

THE AFTERMATH OF AMERICA'S FIRST HIGH-PROFILE SCHOOL SHOOTING

Tamara Jones

Tamara Jones, a staff writer for the *Washington Post,* recounts the events of January 29, 1979, when sixteen-year-old Brenda Spencer opened fire on the school yard of Grover Cleveland Elementary School in San Diego, California. By the time the standoff ended, Jones reports, the school's principal and custodian were dead, and one policeman and eight children were wounded. The writer traces the lives and the hardships of the survivors and examines their reactions to the string of school shootings that has plagued America since 1996.

The small bronze plaque can be found at the foot of the flagpole, where it stands in mute and largely forgotten testimony to two men who died, it says, "in the service of helping others." There is no mention of the nine survivors who fell wounded on that violent morning in 1979, and the incident has no name. There was no sense, at the time, that a certain history was being made, that what happened here would prove to be a harbinger of a nation's anguish and horror. It seems an incongruous place to find such a memorial, near sandboxes and a jungle gym, for this bloodsoaked ground was not a battlefield at all, but an elementary school.

The headlines and news bulletins have become numbingly familiar by now: Pearl, Mississippi; Paducah, Kentucky; Jonesboro, Arkansas; Springfield, Oregon. School shootings around the United States have killed at least fourteen people and wounded more than forty in the last twelve months alone. Hit lists of teachers and classmates are circulated at middle schools, and deadly weapons are confiscated from book bags and lockers. What was once unimaginable—that a school, society's ultimate sanctuary, could become a killing field—is now a grim reality.

The Shootings in San Diego
That wasn't the case on January 29, 1979, when Grover Cleveland Elementary became the target in the country's first high-profile school shooting, ground zero in an undeclared war in which children shoot

Excerpted from "Looking Back in Sorrow," by Tamara Jones, *Good Housekeeping,* November 1998. Reprinted with permission from the author.

children. The morning school bell had just rung in the quiet San Diego suburb, and children were trickling into their classrooms when a 16-year-old girl named Brenda Spencer took aim through the telescopic sight of her .22-caliber rifle from her house across the street.

Principal Burton Wragg was in the front office having a last cup of coffee with sixth-grade teacher Daryl Barnes when they heard what sounded like firecrackers going off outside. "Pop, pop, pop" is how Barnes remembers it. Wragg charged out the front door while Barnes headed for a side door to investigate. As Barnes looked toward the front of the school, he saw Wragg stooping over a crying child on the ground. Suddenly, the principal spun around and fell backwards into some bushes, a red stain spreading across his chest. Barnes grabbed a couple of children and herded them into the office, shouting at the secretary to call the police. He rushed back outside to pick up another fallen child and heard three more shots ring out, realizing as he scrambled back to safety that he was now in the sniper's sights. As Barnes tried to calm the panicky children, he spotted custodian Mike Suchar with a blanket in his hand, running toward Wragg. "Before I could scream a warning, he spun. I heard him say, 'My God, I've been hit,' before he fell. Then a whole carload of children came up, and I was screaming, Get the car out of here, get out!" The car screeched away.

Several miles away, in the intensive care unit (ICU) of Alvarado Hospital, the young charge nurse, Joyce Warren, heard the alarm go off for a "Code Blue"—an external disaster. She called dispatch and was stunned to hear the news: There had been a shooting at an elementary school, and casualties were expected. As police barricaded the neighborhood and deployed the SWAT team, reporters from the local newspaper began calling residences nearby. By chance, they reached Brenda Spencer, who readily admitted she was the one firing at the school; the rifle, they would later learn, had been a Christmas gift from her father. When asked why she was doing it, Brenda replied matter-of-factly: "I don't like Mondays. This livens up the day." By the time it was all over, Wragg and Suchar were dead, and a policeman and eight children were wounded.

The smallest victims are grown now, their lives changed irrevocably. Dwindling enrollment forced the school to close years ago, and the district currently uses it for workshops. Brenda Spencer has reached adulthood behind bars and is next eligible for parole in 2001. Each time another school comes under siege, the unanswered questions are asked yet again: Why is this happening? How can it be stopped?

Cam Miller

On that January day, DeLois Miller was dropping off her 9-year-old son, Cam, on her way to work. Normally, she let the fourth grader out at Cleveland's side gate, on the upper playground, but it was unusually cold that morning, so she drove Cam around to the front. She vaguely heard what sounded like a car backfiring as she pulled away. Christy Buell, another 9-year-old, had walked the couple of blocks to school. Her widowed father had toyed with the idea of letting Christy and her siblings play hookey that day so the family could drive to the snow-covered mountains, but had thought better of it. Now Christy was playing slip-and-slide on the frosty grass with a friend before the final bell. She heard a popping noise. "All of a sudden, it felt like my whole body was falling asleep," she remembers, "like pinpricks all over. We just heard someone shouting, 'Run! Run!' I crawled up the pathway to the speech room. The teacher heard me crying and opened the door and pulled me in, and two more bullets whizzed by overhead into the door. I don't remember her name, but she saved my life."

Cam Miller was bewildered. Right after his mother dropped him off, he felt something like an electric shock next to his heart. He blacked out briefly. A 7-year-old girl saw him stumble and led him around the corner to a teacher. Cam saw Wragg and Suchar lying on the ground and thought, with childlike logic, that if he could just make it out of that square of sidewalk, "it will all go away."

It never did.

Today, Cam Miller is a handsome 29-year-old, a strapping man with scant resemblance to the chubby-cheeked boy with a bowl hair-cut whose class picture appeared in the newspaper above the word victim. Wearing jeans with a white sweatshirt that covers the fading scar a mere inch from his heart, he sits in the pristine living room of the house he and his wife bought recently, about a half-hour's drive from his childhood home. "I moved up here and I know, well, I think she wouldn't be able to find me," Cam explains. Brenda Spencer's father still lives across the street from the old school, and if Brenda were ever paroled, Cam figures, that is where she would return.

The bullet struck Cam in the back and exited his chest, missing any internal organs. Because he never had a chance to defend himself, however futilely, Cam grew up with an overwhelming fear of leaving his back exposed. "If I go somewhere like a restaurant, I have to sit where I can avoid having my back to the window," he says. As a child, he suffered terrifying nightmares of Brenda Spencer "popping out of the bathtub to finish me off." For a couple of months, he would wake up his mother once a night and have her walk him around the house to the back, where there was a wall of windows. Cam would insist on touching each pane of glass to assure himself that none was broken, that "she" hadn't slipped inside. "The fear I had was that I never saw her," he says. He was wearing a brand-new blue down vest and a matching shirt the day he was shot. Blue was Brenda Spencer's favorite color, he later heard. Blue made him a target. Even now, Cam Miller does not wear blue shirts.

He has seen Brenda Spencer a few times: first, from his hospital bed, as he watched the television news which showed police leading away a petite, freckled girl with long red hair and aviator glasses. Later, Cam went with his parents to court. The judge and marshals took Cam aside beforehand and told the little boy what to expect: She would be handcuffed, they assured him; he would be safe. "When I saw her, the look she gave me—her whole appearance was very evil and scary. She looked like the devil. Blank, empty stare. She just sat there and glared at me."

Brenda Spencer's Troubled Personality

Brenda pleaded guilty to two counts of first-degree murder, eight counts of assault with a deadly weapon, and one count of assault on a peace officer. She was sentenced to twenty-five years to life in prison. Because there was no trial, few details about her family or her past came to light. The Spencers were divorced; Brenda and her older brother lived with their father. Kids in the neighborhood would later say Brenda had a reputation for torturing cats and had dug a series of tunnels in her backyard; adults would describe her as quiet and a loner. The year before the shooting, Brenda and a friend were caught vandalizing Cleveland Elementary—throwing paint in classrooms, overturning desks—but the incident was treated as a typical juvenile prank.

The San Diego County district attorney's (DA) office, whose investigation of Brenda Spencer eventually filled dozens of boxes, privately concluded that she was a sociopath. "We interviewed a friend of hers who admitted the two of them had been planning to kill someone for some time," says Andrea Crisanti, the deputy DA currently assigned to monitor the case in the event Brenda requests parole. "They decided they wanted to kill a cop, to see what that would feel like. Their first plan was to go up to a policeman sitting in a patrol car, and Brenda would go to the passenger window and distract him, and the friend would take Brenda's .22 and shoot him from the driver's side. Then they thought maybe they'd handcuff him to the steering wheel and shoot him with his own service revolver. Then they decided they would lure him into a public rest room—throw eggs at the car or something—and swing an ax and kill him there. This is the mind-set of Brenda Spencer."

Brenda has come up for parole twice, most recently in January 1998. The district attorney's office contacted the victims it was able to locate and told them they could write impact statements. Cam decided to deliver his in person. He and his wife drove the hour and a half to the women's prison in the California desert, arriving much too early. "I was psyching myself up," Cam says. Once there, Brenda, on the advice of her attorney, decided to withdraw her bid for parole. "My wife saw her through the window and said, 'There she is.'" By the time Cam looked, he saw only her retreating back and a glimpse of her red hair. He felt cheated. He had wanted to confront her, finally. There were questions he meant to ask: How could you do something like that? Why do you think you deserve a second chance when the principal and custodian can't have a second chance? Why didn't you just pull the gun on yourself?

Cam is a probation officer now. He conducts jailhouse interviews and prepares presentencing reports that help determine punishment for criminals. When another school shooting is on the evening news, he finds himself watching for the fearful faces of young survivors. "I think it's really sad all those kids are going to have to go through what I've gone through all my life," he says. Although the school offered counseling to the children at the time, Cam never went, and the shooting was a subject his parents couldn't bear to discuss, relying on time and their faith to heal the wounds.

Flashbacks

But even now, DeLois Miller chokes up retelling the story. When two heavily armed boys in Jonesboro, Arkansas, ambushed their classmates, when a teenage boy in Springfield, Oregon, raked his high school cafeteria with gunfire, whenever it happens again, Miller suffers flashbacks, "and I can feel what those other parents are going through." She returns to the old neighborhood occasionally and walks back up the pathway where she dropped Cam off that morning. Two small trees were planted in memory of the principal and custodian, she notes, and over the years they have grown, like her son, tall and strong.

In Kathe Wragg's backyard, there are trees heavy with unplucked fruit. Loquat, persimmon, tangerine, apple, orange, plum, apricot, peach. The yard was Burt's pride and joy. He could make anything grow. A frustrated farmer, he even kept hens so the family would have fresh eggs for breakfast. Kathe and Burt met when both were young teachers in San Diego. They'd known each other only a few months when he proposed on New Year's Eve. Kathe said she'd have to think about it for a day. "He had such an upset stomach, he told me, he couldn't sleep that night, not knowing what would happen. But of course I did say yes." When the babies came along, two sons and a daughter, Kathe stopped working. The family loved to go camping, and Burt had built a dune buggy with a Flintstones top so they could all race across the Anza-Borrego desert and count the stars at night.

In the fall of 1978, Burt took the job as principal at Cleveland Elementary. The school was just a short drive from his hilltop home. On the morning of January 29, 1979, he left, as usual, around 7:00 A.M. "I remember he was wearing a new shirt," Kathe says. Their oldest child, Penny, was in college and living on her own; Penny and Burt had spent the weekend painting her old room. Now Kathe began tidying up the mess. She had the Phil Donahue Show on in the background. A news flash came across the screen. "I can still see it: Sniper attack at Cleveland Elementary School," Kathe says. It didn't fully register. "I thought, Oh my gosh, that's Burt's school. Burt'll take care of it." Minutes later, a neighbor whose husband was on the SWAT team came by. Burt had been shot, she told Kathe. The Wraggs' sons, both in high school, were being taken to Alvarado Hospital by their principal, and Penny was on her way too. At the hospital, Kathe was ushered into a quiet room.

"When I first talked to the nurse, I could see it in her face. I wanted to know if he suffered." Burt had been shot once through the aorta and died in the operating room. Tom, the middle child and older son, had "the worst time of it, I know, because he cried every night for three months," Kathe recalls. His father was killed just a few days before his seventeenth birthday; what was supposed to be a party became a wake. Kathe knew she had to steel herself. "I told myself, I just have to get a handle on this fast. I'm not going to be an emotional cripple. I'm going to accept this, because there's nothing I can do."

Two weeks before he died, Burt got up early on a Saturday morning, as he usually did, to put on the coffee and feed his hens. He and Kathe sat in the kitchen of the slumbering house, enjoying their private time. Kathe felt tremendous peace. "If I would die tomorrow, I would think it had all been just wonderful," she told her husband. Burt agreed.

Moving On

It took Kathe six months to face the task of clearing out Burt's belongings. She kept his wedding suit, a pen holder, and a painting some teachers had given him, an acrylic that reminds her of their trip to Newfoundland. "It took years to cut down on the groceries," she says. She wrapped herself in the protective cocoon of their many friends, "because I didn't want to be alone, ever." She hired a gardener to tend to the trees but let Burt's vegetable garden go barren. She keeps busy with volunteer work and travel. She dates, but she's never found anyone to love the way she did Burt.

When strangers meet her, they sometimes recognize her name and feel compelled to tell her where they were, what they were doing, on the morning of the shooting, as if time had stood still. Kathe herself wonders what ever became of Cleveland's children, the ones she still thinks of as "Burt's kids." Widowed barely two weeks, she took Valentine's Day candy and cards to those who were hospitalized, and visited the school to try to assure the children that everything would be all right. She has seen the spot where Burt was gunned down, "because I needed to see it." It made her feel empty.

There are six grandchildren now, and they sometimes ask what happened to Grandpa. Kathe tells them the truth. The first time Brenda Spencer came up for parole, Kathe was never officially notified; she heard the news from a reporter who called for comment. She has since made it a point to track the case; when the hearing date was scheduled in 1998, Kathe and her brother wrote impact statements. In hers, Kathe called Brenda "a pathetic, self-absorbed, bored, and uncaring thrill seeker" whose cowardly act left innocent families devastated. Life in prison, Kathe feels, is too lenient. "Isn't it funny? I don't feel anger as such," she insists, her blue eyes bright and piercing. "I dissociate myself. I can't control her. I can only control myself."

Kathe lives by herself in the old house, but she is not afraid. "I feel so safe. I kind of feel somebody watching over me." She vividly remembers hearing soft footfalls in the hall one night. "And I was thinking, Oh, you're back." In the sunroom, she is working on a jigsaw puzzle, which she finds soothing, the way all the pieces fit so predictably together.

The Scene at the Hospital

Children shot. The words still make Joyce Warren shake her head. She is 56 now, the mother of three sons, still a charge nurse in the ICU at Alvarado Hospital, which in 1979 was little more than a community hospital and today is a large medical center.

The scene at the hospital that day was bedlam. Children were crying; others were too traumatized to even whimper. Hysterical parents began filling the hallway, shouting out names, demanding to know if their children were there. Warren tried to keep everyone calm. As soon as his mother arrived, Cam Miller wanted to know about the custodian, Mike Suchar. "Mom, he's dead, isn't he?" Cam asked; his mother didn't know. "Mom, I know he's dead," Cam insisted. "I was in the same ambulance." Suchar's body had rolled onto Cam when the ambulance raced around a curve. Cam thought that meant he might die too.

Of the injured, Cam was one of the luckier ones. At least three children had abdominal wounds, and a young policeman who had tried to get to Burton Wragg was shot in the neck and narrowly missed being paralyzed. After police arrived at the school, Brenda Spencer barricaded herself inside the house for more than six hours; when she finally surrendered, police found more than 200 rounds of ammunition in the house, which investigators described as filthy. During the siege, police commandeered a garbage truck and parked it in front of the Spencer house, trying to block the school from Brenda's line of fire. While buses evacuated the school from the back, police carried injured children to ambulances in the front. Christy Buell was the most seriously hurt, shot through the abdomen and in the buttocks. At Alvarado, she was whisked off to surgery. Doctors removed the bullet and repaired her intestine.

Christy's father paced the hallway with one of her dolls. "I knew the hospital routine," Norm Buell, now 63, says. He had lost his wife to leukemia when Christy was 3. The teacher who had dragged Christy inside to safety that morning would later tell investigators how the little girl had kept sobbing out the same words, over and over: "I want my daddy, I want my daddy."

A Terrible Anger

In the ICU, Joyce Warren surveyed the tiny bodies on stretchers and had to fight to maintain her professional detachment: That could be my child, she thought. "Today, every time I read one of those articles about another shooting, it takes me back to that day. At the time, I didn't think it would happen again." Joyce is taking a quick break on the hospital's patio, dressed in a lilac top with a cheery daisy-covered smock over slacks. "Violence seems to be escalating in young children," she observes. "There seems to be this terrible anger, almost a hopelessness. We need to be trying to teach people to teach their children the value of a life."

Daryl Barnes agrees. Now 57, he teaches at another elementary school. "I remember a boy came to school with a .22 pistol. Had the gun in a backpack," Barnes says. "He was ten or eleven. They suspended him, slapped his hand a bit. I'm kind of old-school, and I believe we have rules and standards and there have to be consequences. If young people start making adult-type decisions, there should be adult-type consequences. People make choices." Still, Barnes adds, "a gun in the hands of a child is a poor choice by an adult."

The Brenda Spencers have lost their shock value for him now; he views violent children as the inevitable result of larger societal problems. "Everybody has their agenda, but I'm not sure the children are the most important thing anymore. We had an open house recently at my school. There are thirty-five kids in my class. Only twelve parents showed up." Strict regulations and fear of lawsuits have made disciplining troublemakers nearly impossible, Barnes adds, "and teachers tend to be afraid to take a strong stand."

The father of four children who are now grown, Barnes remembers coming home late the evening of the Cleveland shooting and finding them all waiting for him in front of the TV in the living room. "We talked about it as a family," he says, "and we just went on with our lives. That's what we tried to do at the school too. They brought in counselors from everywhere and encouraged the kids and teachers to talk about it." Barnes did not seek counseling after the Cleveland shooting but says, "Looking back, I see I should have." The Jonesboro incident in particular brought back sharp memories. "It's going to keep happening, till somebody takes responsibility. Because they're children and people revere children, it's hard to bring heavy consequences."

Acting on Red Flags

He forgives Brenda Spencer, he says, but believes "she's where she belongs for the rest of her life." Barnes's classroom was one of the rooms Brenda had vandalized the year before the shooting. Suddenly he remembers something about that episode: "I never told anyone about this before; I forgot about it completely until now. There was a picture of me in the room—a class picture, I guess it was—and evidently they had a BB gun, because someone had shot a hole straight through my forehead."

Even when red flags are apparent, acting on them can be problematic. At the San Diego DA's office, Andrea Crisanti and her colleagues sometimes find themselves debating: If DNA testing could tell you which child was going to be a sociopath, even with that certainty, what would you do? Crisanti cites a recent case involving a brutal 24-year-old killer whose troubled childhood was carefully documented by teachers and counselors—uncontrollable rage, repeated fights, lack of empathy for others. "When this kid was eight years old, his teacher wrote in his file: 'If looks could kill, I'd be dead a thousand times.' This was when he was eight! He was a ticking time bomb waiting to go off."

The prosecutor, herself the mother of three young children, can quote from memory the words of one of Brenda Spencer's victims: "I felt a sting in my tummy and then I got sort of dizzy and I got tired so I laid down and then Mr. Wragg came up and he was talking to me and then Mr. Wragg jumped back into the bushes and then he laid down there and just kind of died." Her dusty files also contain the words of Brenda Spencer at the time, boasting about how easy it was to shoot children, that she liked to watch them squirm, and especially liked shooting the ones wearing down jackets so she could watch the feathers fly. "I don't know that she's ever expressed true remorse," Crisanti says. "I just look at her picture and I see empty. You think: I can't see a soul. There's nothing in there."

Nor does she have any answers. "You just constantly have to be aware of what your kids are listening to and watching—they pick up on incredible violence that we all know is in records and videos. You have to pay attention to who they associate with. Now it's not a question of whether it will happen again, but where."

When another school shooting is in the news, Daryl Barnes shares the story of what happened at Cleveland with his fifth graders, hoping the horror will make an impression on their young minds. He went back to the old school not long ago, for a teachers' workshop. "At the break, I found myself out by the flagpole," he recalls, "just looking at the plaque."

"Part of My Life"

Christy Buell never left the neighborhood. Now 29, she is a sunny preschool teacher with lovely, startling green eyes and the kind of determination that helped her lose more than 100 pounds a year ago by walking up and down a mountain near her home. She lives with her father and brother in the house she grew up in and is reluctant, at first, to talk about the shooting, because she considers it just some-thing that happened, "part of my life," and she has moved on. She keeps a scrapbook of newspaper articles and photos, and still has the jacket she wore that day stashed away somewhere. "Six months after I got my jacket back, I found a hole in the hood," she recalls, surmising that a third bullet passed through it without hitting her. Her memo-ries form a terrible collage: the principal moaning in the sticker bush; doctors cutting off her bloody Winnie-the-Pooh shirt; being unable to open her eyes until she heard her father's voice.

Christy had a colostomy for two months and was unable to return to school that year. Nerve damage left her leg paralyzed for a while, and she wore a brace: there was one to walk in ("I called that one the clicker because of the sound it made"), one to sleep in, and one that fit around her calf so she could wear shoes. She was in the hospital for forty-two days and underwent two operations. When she came home, the living room was filled with mounds of toys and games from well-wishers around the world. The police chief visited and gave her a pin in the shape of handcuffs. The jeweler whose store was a few doors down from the Buells' restaurant sent Christy a diamond-chip ring. Her father insisted Christy choose three or four favorite toys and donate the rest to a home for abused and neglected children.

"We just kind of went on with life," Christy remembers. "Dad did-n't want me to see a psychologist. He just said we'd deal with it as a family. Dad set the direction, and I took the path. We talk about it all the time. It's an incident that will never leave my mind. I'm not trau-matized for life or anything. If I hear a loud bang or a car backfire, it gets my heart beating, but that's about it."

Still, she finds herself thinking about it in the abstract at the preschool where she teaches, especially when she's outside with the children. "I have often had visions of it happening there, and I think about what I'd be doing if it did happen." Mentally she plots an escape route, how she will get the children to safety. The sandbox, she thinks; she will push them to the ground in the sandbox and shield them. Not long after Brenda Spencer went to jail, Wallace Spencer, her father, married her 17-year-old cellmate. They had a child together, and the little girl attended Christy's preschool. She resembled Brenda, Christy noticed. Christy would see Wallace Spencer occasionally when he came to pick up the child. Sometimes he would say hello, and Christy would politely answer, uncertain whether he realized who she was. One day, the little girl announced to Christy, "My sis-ter's in jail." Christy mustered a benign response: "Oh, really?"

"A Cry for Help"

It bothers her that Brenda Spencer never has accepted responsibility; she has at various times alleged that police SWAT team members actu-ally shot the children, or that she was on hallucinogenic drugs at the time and prosecutors faked a clean toxicology report, or that she didn't understand the guilty plea when she signed it. Christy herself grew up in a home with guns, "but they were always locked up, and we couldn't get to them." Her father taught her to shoot when she was around 12 or 13, but "he taught us right and wrong. People should talk to their kids more, find out what's going on in their lives, and if you hear anything remotely strange, don't pass it up just because your life is busy. Talk to them about the safety of guns."

Norm Buell took Christy out target shooting a couple of months after she got home from the hospital. "I didn't want her to fear weapons," he says now. "I wanted her to understand that they're to be respected." He believes that when Brenda Spencer pulled the trigger "it was a frustrated cry for help. . . . She still probably can't tell you why she did it."

For almost twenty years now, Wallace Spencer has maintained a public silence about his daughter's crime. He and his ex-wife have attended Brenda's parole hearings, and prison authorities say Brenda receives occasional visits from members of her family. A couple of months after the shooting, Norm Buell found himself on Wallace Spencer's front doorstep. "I went over there father-to-father, hoping to talk to him. I wanted to tell him that I was a single father, too, raising four kids alone, and I know it's a hard job and a thankless job, and that I know he probably did the best he could, and that Christy was going to be okay." He could see Spencer through the screen door, sitting in front of the TV. "He wouldn't talk to me," Buell remembers. "He said to go away, and I respected that." He has long since lost his sympathy for the man. When another neighborhood is on the evening news, and he sees the stunned faces of parents in Jonesboro or Springfield or Pearl or Paducah, Norm Buell finds himself hungry for any scrap of information about the families of the children who kill, hoping, as he still does with Brenda Spencer, to make some sense of it.

Down the familiar street, the flag in front of Cleveland Elementary stirs just slightly in the breeze, and the sun glints off the tiny bronze plaque commemorating the bloodshed that was never supposed to happen again. The school itself seems bleak and forgotten, the laughter of its children long silent.

CHAPTER 2

THE CAUSES OF
SCHOOL VIOLENCE

Contemporary Issues
Companion

THE LINK BETWEEN PSYCHIATRIC DRUGS AND SCHOOL SHOOTINGS

Kelly Patricia O'Meara

Kelly Patricia O'Meara, a reporter for *Insight on the News*, explains the possible link between the rise in mass shootings in America's schools and the increase in prescriptions of psychotropic drugs for young people. She points out that many of the perpetrators of the high-profile massacres that occurred in U.S. schools between 1996 and 1999 were taking the psychotropic drugs Ritalin, Prozac, or Luvox. According to O'Meara, these drugs have been known to cause psychotic episodes and violent behavior in some patients and may therefore have played a part in causing these perpetrators to take violent action. Despite the known negative effects that prescription psychiatric drugs can have on children, O'Meara states, they continue to be prescribed at an alarmingly high rate.

Just three weeks after Eric Harris and Dylan Klebold went on their April 20, 1999, killing spree at Columbine High School in Littleton, Colorado, President Clinton hosted a White House conference on youth violence. The president declared it a strategy session to seek "the best ideas from people who can really make a difference: parents and young people, teachers and religious leaders, law enforcement, gun manufacturers, representatives of the entertainment industry and those of us here in government."

There was, however, complete silence from the president when it came to including representatives from the mental-health community, whom many believe can provide important insight about the possible connection between the otherwise seemingly senseless acts of violence being committed by school-age children and prescription psychotropic drugs such as Ritalin, Luvox and Prozac.

There are nearly 6 million children in the United States between the ages of 6 and 18 taking mind-altering drugs prescribed for alleged mental illnesses that increasing numbers of mental-health professionals are questioning.

Excerpted from "Doping Kids," by Kelly Patricia O'Meara, *Insight*, June 28, 1999. Copyright ©1999 by News World Communications, Inc. Reprinted with permission from *Insight*. All rights reserved.

Prescription Drugs and Violent Behavior

Although the list of school-age children who have gone on violent rampages is growing at a disturbing rate—and the shootings at Columbine became a national wake-up call—few in the mental-health community have been willing to talk about the possibility that the heavily prescribed drugs and violence may be linked. Those who try to investigate quickly learn that virtually all data concerning violence and psychotropic drugs are protected by the confidentiality provided minors. But in the highly publicized shootings that occurred between 1998 and 1999, information has been made available to the public.

• *April 16, 1999:* Shawn Cooper, a 15-year-old sophomore at Notus Junior-Senior High School in Notus, Idaho, was taking Ritalin, the most commonly prescribed stimulant for bipolar disorder, when he fired two shotgun rounds, narrowly missing students and school staff.

• *April 20, 1999:* Eric Harris, an 18-year-old senior at Columbine High School, killed a dozen students and a teacher before taking his own life. Prior to the shooting rampage, he had been under the influence of Luvox, one of the new selective serotonin reuptake inhibitor, or SSRI, antidepressants approved in 1997 by the Food and Drug Administration, or FDA, for children up to the age of 17 for treatment of obsessive-compulsive disorder, or OCD.

• *May 20, 1999:* T.J. Solomon, a 15-year-old at Heritage High School in Conyers, Ga., was being treated with Ritalin for depression when he opened fire on and wounded six classmates.

Two other high-profile cases from 1998 show a similar pattern:

• *May 21, 1998:* Kip Kinkel, a 15-year-old at Thurston High School in Springfield, Ore., murdered his parents and then proceeded to school where he opened fire on students in the cafeteria, killing two and wounding 22. Kinkel had been prescribed both Ritalin and Prozac. Although widely used among adults, Prozac has not been approved by the FDA for pediatric use.

• *March 24, 1998:* Mitchell Johnson, 13, and Andrew Golden, 11, opened fire on their classmates at Westside Middle School in Jonesboro, Ark. Johnson had been receiving psychiatric counseling and, although information about the psychotropic drugs that may have been prescribed for him has not been made public, his attorney, Val Price, responded when asked about it: "I think that is confidential information, and I don't want to reveal that."

A great deal has been written about all of these cases. There have, however, been no indications that all of these children watched the same TV programs or listened to the same music. Nor has it been established that they all used illegal drugs, suffered from alcohol abuse or had common difficulties with their families or peers. They did not share identical home lives, dress alike or participate in similar extracurricular activities. But all of the above were labeled as suffering from a mental illness and were being treated with psychotropic drugs that for years have been known to cause serious adverse effects when given to children.

Attention-Deficit/Hyperactivity Disorder

At the top of the list of so-called "mental illnesses" among children is attention-deficit/hyperactivity disorder, or ADHD, which is diagnosed when a child meets six of the 18 criteria described in the *Diagnostic and Statistical Manual of Mental Disorders*, or *DSM-IV*, published by the American Psychiatric Association, or APA.

ADHD was determined by a vote of APA psychiatrists to be a "mental" illness and added to the *DSM-IIIR* in 1987. By definition, children with ADHD exhibit behaviors such as not paying attention in school, not listening when spoken to directly, failing to follow directions, losing things, being easily distracted and forgetful, fidgeting with hands or feet, talking excessively, blurting out answers or having difficulty awaiting turn. The most common ADHD remedy among pediatricians and representatives of the mental-health community is, as noted, Ritalin.

First approved by the Food and Drug Administration (FDA) in 1955, Ritalin (methylphenidate) had become widely used for behavioral control by the mid-1960s. It is produced by the Swiss pharmaceutical company Novartis. According to the Drug Enforcement Administration, or DEA, the United States buys and uses 90 percent of the world's Ritalin. A U.N. agency known as the International Narcotics Control Board, or INCB, reported in 1995 that "10 to 12 percent of all boys between the ages of 6 and 14 in the U.S. have been diagnosed as having ADD [attention-deficit disorder, now referred to as ADHD] and are being treated with methylphenidate."

But opponents are concerned about evidence they say confirms a close relationship between use of prescribed psychotropic drugs and subsequent use of illegal drugs, including cocaine and heroin. While the United States has spent more than $70 billion on the war on drugs, says Bruce Wiseman, president of the Citizens Commission on Human Rights, a California-based organization that investigates violations of human rights by mental-health practitioners, "if you think the Colombian drug cartel is the biggest drug dealer in the world, think again. It's your neighborhood psychiatrist . . . putting our kids on the highest level of addictive drugs."

This complaint is not new and there is a lengthy list of government agencies connecting the prescribed psychotropic drugs to use of illegal substances.

Twenty-eight years ago the World Health Organization, or WHO, concluded that Ritalin was pharmacologically similar to cocaine in its pattern of abuse and cited Ritalin as a Schedule II drug—the most addictive in medical usage. The Department of Justice followed the WHO by citing Ritalin in Schedule II of the Controlled Substances Act as having a very high potential for abuse. As a Schedule II drug,

Ritalin joins morphine, opium, cocaine and the heroin substitute methadone.

According to a report in the 1995 *Archives of General Psychiatry*, "Cocaine is one of the most reinforcing and addicting of the abused drugs and has pharmacological actions that are very similar to those of Ritalin." In the same year the DEA also made the Ritalin/cocaine connection, saying, "It is clear that Ritalin substitutes for cocaine and d-amphetamine in a number of behavioral paradigms," expressing concern that "one in every 30 Americans between 5 and 19 years old has a prescription for the drug."

Despite decades of warnings about the potential for abuse of Ritalin, experts continue to argue that the benefits far outweigh the consequences. Yet the INCB has reported that "Methylphenidate's [Ritalin] pharmacological effects are essentially the same as those of amphetamine and methamphetamine. The abuse of methylphenidate [Ritalin] can lead to tolerance and severe psychological dependence. Psychotic episodes [and] violent and bizarre behavior have been reported."

These are, in fact, some of the same symptoms exhibited by Eric Harris.

David Fassler, a child and adolescent psychiatrist and chairman of the APA group on Children, Adolescents and Their Families, says he is unaware of any research to suggest a correlation between the recent cases of violent behavior in school-age children and the widespread prescription of psychotropic drugs. Fassler argues that the number of school-age children suffering from mental illnesses such as depression is "more than earlier believed and it is important that there be a comprehensive evaluation by a mental-health clinician trained in this area." He stresses that "treatment should be multimodal—not left to medications alone."

Mike Faenza, president and chief executive officer of the National Mental Health Association, the country's oldest and largest mental-health group, notes that "there is little known about how the drugs affect brain function." Faenza adds that "we do know that a hell of a lot of kids commit suicide because they aren't getting the help they need. It's irresponsible not to give them the help just because we don't know what causes the mental illness."

"A Contrived Epidemic"

Opponents are quick to capitalize on this admission. "There is no such thing as ADHD," declares Wiseman. "It's not a deficiency of 'speed' that makes a kid act out. If you look at the criteria listed in the *DSM-IV* for ADHD, you'll see that they are taking normal childhood behavior and literally voting it a mental illness. This is a pseudoscience, entirely subjective. Unlike medical conditions that are proved scientifically, with these mental illnesses the only way you know you're better is if the psychiatrist says you're better. That's not science."

Pediatric neurologist Fred Baughman not only agrees that there is no such illness as ADHD, but says: "This is a contrived epidemic, where all 5 million to 6 million children on these drugs are normal. The country's been led to believe that all painful emotions are a mental illness and the leadership of the APA knows very well that they are representing it as a disease when there is no scientific data to confirm any mental illness."

Peter Breggin, a psychiatrist and director of the International Center for the Study of Psychiatry and Psychology and author of *Talking Back to Prozac, Toxic Psychiatry* and *Talking Back to Ritalin*, for years has waged a war with the APA about what he regards as its cavalier diagnoses of mental illnesses. "Psychiatry has never been driven by science. They have no biological or genetic basis for these illnesses and the National Institutes of Mental Health are totally committed to the pharmacological line." He is concerned that "there is a great deal of scientific evidence that stimulants cause brain damage with long-term use, yet there is no evidence that these mental illnesses, such as ADHD, exist."

Breggin points out that the National Institutes of Health, or NIH, admitted as much at their 1998 Consensus Development Conference on the Diagnosis and Treatment of Attention Deficit Hyperactivity Disorder. Thirty-one individuals were selected by NIH to make scientific presentations to the panel on ADHD and its treatment. The panel made the following observations and conclusions: "We don't have an independent, valid test for ADHD; there are no data to indicate that ADHD is due to a brain malfunction; existing studies come to conflicting conclusions as to whether use of psychostimulants increases or decreases the risk of abuse, and finally after years of clinical research and experience with ADHD, our knowledge about the cause or causes of ADHD remains speculative."

The Side Effects of Psychotropic Drugs

If so, there is little evidence to support a scientific basis for classifying ADHD as a mental illness. On the other hand, there is an abundance of evidence that stimulants such as Ritalin can produce symptoms such as mania, insomnia, hallucinations, hyperactivity, impulsivity and inattention. And the DEA's list of potentially adverse effects of Ritalin includes psychosis, depression, dizziness, insomnia, nervousness, irritability and attacks of Tourette's or other tic syndromes.

While Ritalin is the drug of choice for treating ADHD, other mental illnesses such as depression and obsessive-compulsive disorder, or OCD, from which Columbine shooter Harris suffered, are being treated with new SSRI antidepressants. Harris' autopsy revealed that he had used Luvox (Fluvoxomine), an SSRI, prior to the shooting spree. And days earlier he had been rejected by the Marine Corps because he was taking the psychotropic drug.

Luvox, a cousin of Prozac, has been approved by the FDA for pediatric use, although research shows that a small percentage of patients experience adverse effects such as mania, bouts of irritability, aggression and hostility. But many physicians still prescribe it to children.

More disturbing to those who believe sufficient evidence exists that prescription psychotropic drugs may play a role in the violence being carried out by school-age children is the response of physicians to the issue. Rather than erring on the side of caution by reducing the number of kids on mind-altering drugs, physicians instead are prescribing psychotropic drugs even to infants and toddlers. The warning label states that "Ritalin should not be used in children under 6 years, since safety and efficacy for this age group has not been established" and "sufficient data on safety and efficacy of long-term use of Ritalin in children are not yet available."

"Fraudulent Diagnoses"

A report in the July 1998 issue of the *Clinical Psychiatric News* revealed that in Michigan's Medicaid program, 223 children 3 years old or younger were diagnosed with ADHD as of December 1996. Amazingly, 57 percent of these children, many of whom are not yet capable of putting together a complete sentence, were treated with one or more psychotropic drugs including Ritalin, Prozac, Dexedrine, Aventyl and Syban. Thirty-three percent were medicated with two or more of these drugs.

But it is Ritalin that is being prescribed to 6 million American children. Children's Hospital in Washington has been running television advertisements expressing concern. According to its spokeswoman, Lynn Cantwell, the ads were part of a series covering many medical issues. "We wanted to advocate that children get a comprehensive evaluation because we are finding that children were coming in who were taking Ritalin who actually did not have ADHD."

Wiseman has suggested that the only way to gain control of the situation is to expose widespread "fraudulent diagnoses" of psychiatrists. "Without the diagnoses, you can't get the drugs," he says. Baughman's answer isn't too far from Wiseman's. He says, "A big-time class-action lawsuit needs to be filed."

THE RELATIONSHIP BETWEEN MEDIA VIOLENCE AND SCHOOL VIOLENCE

William J. Bennett

Countless studies have determined that there is an irrefutable link between violence in the media and violent behavior in children, argues former secretary of education William J. Bennett. In the following selection, adapted from his testimony before the Senate Committee on Commerce on May 4, 1999, Bennett explains the role that media violence may have played in the April 1999 school shooting in Littleton, Colorado, in which Eric Harris and Dylan Klebold killed twelve classmates and a teacher before turning their guns on themselves. While other factors may also have contributed to the massacre at Littleton, Bennett points out that society should not close its eyes to the connection that research has found between violence in the media and violent behavior in young people.

Most of you know that I am a conservative Republican, which I have been for 13 years. But I was also proud to be a Democrat for 22 years. And one of the things proud Democrats do is read the *New Republic*. I still read the *New Republic* occasionally and want to commend an article in its most recent issue by Greg Easterbrook.

Here are the first two paragraphs of the article, which talk about the 1996 slasher/so-called "ironic-comedy" movie, *Scream*. The movie was produced by Disney's Miramax division. Easterbrook writes:

> Millions of teens have seen the 1996 movie *Scream,* a box-office and home-rental hit. Critics adored the film. The *Washington Post* declared that it "deftly mixes irony, self-reference, and social wry commentary." The *Los Angeles Times* hailed it as "a bravura, provocative send-up." *Scream* opens with a scene in which a teenage girl is forced to watch her jock boyfriend tortured and then disemboweled by two fellow students who, it will eventually be learned, want revenge on anyone from high school who crossed them. After jock boy's stomach is shown cut open and he dies screaming, the killers

Excerpted from "Marketing Violence to Children," testimony given by William J. Bennett before the Senate Committee on Commerce, May 4, 1999, Washington, D.C.

stab and torture the girl, then cut her throat and hang her body from a tree so that Mom can discover it when she drives up. A dozen students and teachers are graphically butchered in the film, while the characters make running jokes about murder. At one point, a boy tells a big-breasted friend she'd better be careful because the stacked girls always get it in horror films. In the next scene, she's grabbed, stabbed through the breasts, and murdered. . . . The movie builds to a finale in which one of the killers announces that he and his accomplice started off by murdering strangers but then realized it was a lot more fun to kill their friends.

Mr. Easterbrook goes on to write:

Now that two Colorado high schoolers have murdered twelve classmates and a teacher—often, it appears, first taunting their pleading victims, just like celebrity stars do in the movies!—some commentators have dismissed the role of violence in the images shown to the young. . . . But mass murders by the young, once phenomenally rare, are suddenly on the increase. Can it be coincidence that this increase is happening at the same time that Hollywood has begun to market the notion that mass murder is fun?

Mr. Easterbrook's question is a very good one. According to several accounts, Dylan Klebold and Eric Harris enjoyed killing their classmates and teacher. They laughed and hollered, said one survivor, "like it was, like, exciting."

Klebold, Harris, and Marilyn Manson

According to media reports, it turns out that Klebold and Harris were fans, even devotees, of a lot in our popular culture. Classmates have said that they listened to, among others, the shock rocker Marilyn Manson, who refers to himself as the "God of F***." Manson recently said that "the end of the world is all we have to look forward to—I'm just pushing the fast-forward button and letting you enjoy the ride." People like Manson do not simply rise by themselves out of America's basements; they are bankrolled by some of America's oldest and most respected corporations.

Mr. Chairman, let me here recall a story that I think bears on the subject of today's hearing. In 1995, when Seagram Co. purchased a 50 percent stake in Interscope Records, which included Manson's albums, Edgar Bronfman Jr., the president and CEO of Seagram, called me to request a meeting. I agreed to it, and in January 1996, Bronfman flew to Washington.

Bronfman's purpose was to allay my concerns and to preempt criticisms by me and my colleagues Senator Joseph Lieberman and C. DeLores Tucker of the National Political Congress of Black Women regarding Seagram's purchase. During the meeting, he told me the deal he was making with Interscope would allow him to refuse to distribute music he deemed inappropriate. Bronfman assured me that there were "lines we will not cross," that Seagram would not profit by disseminating objectionable music. "Watch us and judge us," Bronfman said.

I took him at his word. I praised his willingness to make normative judgments and to conclude that some music was beyond the pale. It turns out, however, that either his word that day was no good or his definition of objectionable music is far different from mine. Consider these words from Marilyn Manson's song "Irresponsible Hate Anthem": "Hey, victim, should I black your eyes again?/ Hey, victim,/You were the one who put the stick in my hand/I am the ism, my hate's a prism/Let's just kill everyone and let your God sort them out/F*** it, F*** it, F*** it, F***/Everybody's someone else's nigger. . . ./I wasn't born with enough middle fingers." One of the photos on Manson's *Antichrist Superstar* album pictures Manson's genitals hooked up to a hose which drains into the mouths of two men, kneeling, zombie-like, on either side of him. *Antichrist Superstar* did not disappoint Mr. Bronfman; it rose to Number 3 on the Billboard Album Survey.

Music's Powerful Influence

Seagram, as an industry leader and self-professed setter of standards, should stop its support of lyrics that are unworthy of human consumption. Your colleague Senator Lieberman and I have written letters to Seagram's board of directors and to major stockholders, urging them to use their influence to clean up the music that Seagram distributes. And I have asked Bronfman to publicly debate these issues, in Los Angeles, in New York, anywhere. But so far, all we have heard from one of the world's largest communications corporations and its board is the Sound of Silence.

This is one of the things you should continue to debate: What effect does the popular culture have on the young? In Plato's *Republic,* Socrates said that "musical training is a more potent instrument than any other, because rhythm and harmony find their way into the inward places of the soul, on which they mightily fasten, imparting grace." Rhythm and harmony are still fastening themselves on to children's souls; today, however, much of the music they listen to is imparting mournfulness, darkness, despair, a sense of death.

Mr. Chairman, the events in Littleton were catastrophic for the Columbine students and their families. And it was a horrible moment for this country not just because what happened was so terrible but because it raises questions about key parts of American life. This is a moment that demands hard questions about schools, about parenting, about guns, and about the entertainment industry.

Although today's hearing focuses on the latter, let me say a word about the gun issue and how it relates to what we are talking about. My view on this is that if somebody is a pro-gun ideologue and says "we can't talk about guns in this issue," they do not have much to contribute to this discussion. Similarly, if some shameless Hollywood ideologue says "we can't talk about the influence of movies or television on this," they do not have much to contribute either. In the matter of the protection of our children, nothing should be off-limits. The issue, obviously, involves a bundle of things. We should talk about all of them.

Overwhelming Evidence

Most of us already know that too many of our movies, television shows, music songs, and video games are filled with trash: grisly murder scenes, dismemberment and disembowelment, nonstop profanity, rape and torture scenarios. The relevant questions are: Does it matter and, if it does, how much and what can we do about it?

Almost no one, except for a few blinded by financial stakes, thinks that the popular culture is not having a coarsening effect on our kids. The evidence, empirical and anecdotal, is overwhelming. It is clear, abundant, and it is common-sensical. You will hear some of it today.

Now for some kids—a small percentage—movies, music, television, the Internet make no difference in their lives; they simply are not affected by the stuff. For most kids, however, the popular culture works as a coarsener, desensitizer, and dehumanizer. That is why most parents, although they are not alarmed or revolting in the streets, are deeply worried. They feel as if they are swimming upstream, fighting against faceless television, movie, and music executives who are fighting against them. This is a very serious problem. We should study it and find out more about it.

But another difficulty is in the very small percentage of kids who are, for all intents and purposes, taken over by the popular culture. Who see the violent movies as a game plan. Who hear the dark, pounding music as a hymn. Who are basically severed and metaphysically separated from their parents, families, and communities. Who begin, as Eric Harris and Dylan Klebold did, to live in a dark parallel universe.

Obviously, this is not simply the work of producers or advertisers. But it may be partly the product of their work. If they believe it is not, then the Edgar Bronfmans, Howard Stringers, Michael Eisners, and Oliver Stones [movie producers and directors] of the world should explain why. As you well know, Senators, this is something they have been unwilling to do. . . .

The "Filth Nuts"

I will repeat what I have previously said several times before: I am a virtual absolutist on the First Amendment. All of us have a right to make, produce, and sell *almost* anything we want. But the more important question, at least morally and constitutionally, is not so different from the one asked of gun manufacturers. Should you develop, market, promote, and sell something regardless of how degrading or destructive it is?

If we ask the gun manufacturers to regulate themselves responsibly, which we do (and much more), then at least we should ask the entertainment industry to act responsibly (better than trying to regulate them from Washington). We should ask them what they are doing and why they are doing it. Again, I urge you to take that action. There are some "gun nuts" in the country, of course; now is an appropriate time to uncover the country's "filth nuts." Some will go on to say that as a percentage of all movies, music, and television, the destructive trash is only a small part. I would respond to this claim by pointing out that the gun folks' retort is that only a small percentage of guns are used illegally.

Finally, let me defuse in advance one of my critic's arguments— that we are focusing on the wrong problem when we talk about popular culture since other countries, like Japan, consume the same movies and music that we do but are among the most peaceful nations on earth. Professor Daniel Polsby wrote an article in the *Atlantic Monthly* in which he made the following point: If firearms increase violence and crime, then the rates of violence and crime in Switzerland, New Zealand, and Israel should be higher since their "number of firearms per civilian household is comparable to that in the United States."

The point—and fact—is that we are a complicated country. We are different in many ways from other countries. Our violence is one of those differences. While we are the greatest country in the world, we are also one of its most coarse and most violent. That is not something to celebrate. It is a shame, and needs to be treated that way. By parents, by Congress, and by the entertainment industry.

THE CRUELTY OF HIGH SCHOOL SOCIAL LIFE

Michael Bronski

In the following essay, Michael Bronski, a cultural critic and author, argues that there is a causal connection between violence in schools and the cruel social hierarchy of students. According to Bronski, students who do not fit into the traditionally accepted social roles of preppies, athletes, and cheerleaders are ostracized. These outsiders, he writes, face years of verbal and physical torment that is rarely alleviated because many adults view this practice as harmless teasing, an accepted and unavoidable part of life. Eric Harris and Dylan Klebold, the two students responsible for the April 1999 massacre at Columbine High School in Littleton, Colorado, were considered outsiders in their school and were regularly tormented, Bronski points out. Hopefully, Bronski concludes, the tragedy at Littleton will shed some light on the culture of cruelty that exists among students in U.S. schools.

In April 1999, Eric Harris and Dylan Klebold opened fire on their fellow students at Columbine High School. The funerals are over, the pontificating about "how could this happen" has subsided and while there are ongoing public investigations and panels into whether Hollywood violence transfers from screen to classroom, the press coverage has essentially died down reducing the "Littleton massacre" to tragedy of the week status.

The Harris Suicide Note

Soon after the shootings the *Rocky Mountain News*, a Denver daily printed the suicide note that Eric Harris left at his home explaining his actions. It was picked up by a few news outlets (one of the NPR news shows read parts of it) and probably got its widest circulation when gay advice columnist Dan Savage in the *Stranger,* a progressive free Seattle weekly, reprinted it and it was then syndicated nationally. It read:

> By now, it's over. If you are reading this, my mission is complete. . . . Your children who have ridiculed me, who have

Excerpted from "Littleton, Movies, and Gay Kids," by Michael Bronski, *Z Magazine*, July/August 1999. Reprinted with permission.

chosen not to accept me, who have treated me like I am not worth their time are dead. THEY ARE FUCKING DEAD. . . . Surely you will try to blame it on the clothes I wear, the music I listen to, or the way I choose to present myself, but no. Do not hide behind my choices. You need to face the fact that this comes as a result of YOUR CHOICES. Parents and teachers, you fucked up. You have taught these kids to not accept what is different. YOU ARE IN THE WRONG. I have taken their lives and my own—but it was your doing. Teachers, parents, LET THIS MASSACRE BE ON YOUR SHOULDERS UNTIL THE DAY YOU DIE.

The note is pained and enraged, almost a parody of teen anger and self-involved angst. Its over-the-top apocalyptic tone makes all too real its message of terrible desperation and crazy despair. But if this note "explains" to some degree Harris and Klebold's actions, why didn't it attract more media attention? The answer is, of course, because it did explain their motivation and (at least in the wake of the killings) no one wanted to hear it. It wasn't the popular lament of "how could this happen?" Unanswered questions are often more comforting than the ones that are answered obviously. Some questions are almost never asked. After it was announced that Eric Harris was not accepted into the Marines because he was taking an antidepressant, the press focused on his medication, not whether his desire to join the military had any connection to his violent behavior in school. Hardly anyone mentioned, in the endless wake of outraged articles and editorials about how violent video games were damaging and destroying youth, that many of these games, particularly Doom and Quake, are used by the Marines for training purposes.

Shaping the Story

One can't help but be impressed by how skillfully the reporting shaped the story to fit the preconceived anxieties and biases of a broad readership. From both liberal and conservative vantage points the Columbine High School murders became a Rorschach test of political and social ills: gun control, violent video games, parental responsibility, gothic culture, the dangers of the Internet, racism, heavy metal music, teen angst, white supremacy, Christian evangelicalism, Hitler, athletics, police culpability, and finally—but only after these more incendiary and high-profile issues were played out—the nature and quality of high school culture.

The first waves of reporting and commentary promoted the idea that the Trenchcoat Mafia—the loosely formed and defined group of "outsiders" at Columbine High School of which Eric Harris and Dylan Klebold were ancillary members—was, in essence, a cabal of dangerous, antisocial, Satanist, violence prone, far right-wing thugs.

It looks as though some of the first reporting missed the complexity of the situation. The original charges that Harris and Klebold—and others associated as Trenchcoat Mafia members—wore swastikas or other Nazi symbols were disputed by many Columbine students in later interviews. Similarly, non-white friends of Harris and Klebold contested the idea that they were racist or white supremacist (despite an overtly racist comment Harris made during the shootings).

Being an Outsider

Reading through the follow-up news reports one is struck by small details about the culture of Columbine High, such as more than 60 percent of the students identified as evangelical Christians, wore crosses on chains around their necks and bracelets with the letters "WWJD" ("What Would Jesus Do"). In a telling group interview in the April 30, 1999, edition of the *New York Times* several students discussed race at Columbine and it was shocking to see one of the school's popular jocks (who was white) mention that 200 students out of a total population of 2,000 were African-American. He was corrected by 2 non-white students who said the number was closer to 20, or even 6.

But despite the disinformation and outright untruths that surfaced during the news reporting the one message that has come across is that students identified as "outsiders" have a hard time in high school. This image of the teen outsider is a fairly recent invention and, in the past 50 years, its mythos has changed. Look at Hollywood images from the 1950s when James Dean, Natalie Wood, and Sal Mineo in *Rebel Without a Cause* were portrayed as misunderstood and nearly heroic in their struggles against spirit numbing conformity.

Today any sign of outsider status or inclination is seen as a sign of danger and derangement. When asked by the *New York Times* about the Trenchcoat Mafia, Kevin Koeniger, a popular athlete at Columbine High, replied "If they're different why wouldn't we look at them as weird?" In subsequent interviews Columbine High students complained that Harris, Klebold, and the Trenchcoat Mafia "showed no school spirit." In the aftermath of Littleton there were reports that many schools were beginning to both formally and informally begin "geek profiling"—watching and tracking outsider students of all sorts to spot "trouble." An organization called The National School Safety Center issued a checklist of "dangerous signs" to watch for in kids. It included mood swings, a fondness for violent TV or video games, cursing, depression, antisocial behavior and attitudes. Sound familiar?

Pop Culture's Portrayal of School Cliques

One of the oft-repeated statements in much of the coverage of Littleton is that high school cliques with all of their hierarchies and inequities are inevitable. "There is no way to change this," opined a *New York Times* op-ed, "you can't make cheerleaders get crushes on homely boys." Indeed, the idea that this culture is immutable is entrenched in common thought. It is a never-ending, but trivialized, war: jocks and cheerleaders vs. the nerds, freaks, geeks, and fags. U.S. popular culture has a love/hate relationship with this. For all the films, television shows, and comics that valorize and romanticize the golden boys and girls there are also backlash films. Perhaps no film captures the unleashed rage of the spat-upon as the 1976 *Carrie*— which ends in an apocalyptic firestorm of death that rivals Harris's and Klebold's plans to blow up Columbine High. The 1989 *Heathers* took a more sardonic, smug view of this conflict, but after the popular kids are killed the school still gets blown up. If James Dean and Natalie Wood were misunderstood rebels with a cause who are finally seen as being morally sympathetic in the school world, Sissie Spacek and Christian Slater [the stars of *Carrie* and *Heathers*] were the new outsiders—both with paranormal abilities—who embodied the passion and righteous fury of all out lethal revenge.

But this dichotomy—which alternately represents and sparks the fantasies of both the popular and the disenfranchised—ultimately hides the harsh reality of what happens in high schools. After the first week of coverage students began talking about how "members" of the Trenchcoat Mafia were not only verbally harassed but physically assaulted by the "preps and the athletes." Physically assaulted, in this case, meant being hit in the school hallways, shoved into lockers, having food smashed into their faces in the cafeteria—actions that outside of high school social culture would result in arrest and a possible jail sentence. This violence happens to varying degrees at schools across the country. The tragic irony of "geek profiling" as a way to prevent violence among students is that the violence is—has always been—-already there, and it is generally never perpetrated by geeks.

The Truth Is Addressed

Hopefully, the Littleton catastrophe has begun a more honest, frank public discussion of this violence in U.S. school culture. The *Boston Globe*, the *New York Times*, and other major venues have begun printing articles about violence in middle schools and high schools. Check out Jon Katz's piece "Kids Who Kill" on Slashdot.org and the responses that he has received from students detailing the everyday physical and verbal abuses that they endure—usually at the hands of their more "popular" classmates. One major problem of student on student school violence is that unless the Administration steps in to stop it there is no other alternative but to endure it: you are legally mandated to attend school. Schools, in this situation, become prisons.

The *New York Times* ran "Week in Review" pieces with titles like "Ugly Rites of Passage: Rethinking America's Schools of Hard Knocks." This public discussion is being prompted by a May 24, 1999, Supreme Court ruling *Davis v. Monroe County Board of Education*—holding school districts liable for damages under Federal law for failing to stop a student from subjecting another to severe and pervasive sexual harassment. The Court was bitterly divided with Sandra Day O'Connor, John Paul Stevens, Ruth Bader Ginsburg, Stephen Breyer, and David Souter in the majority and Clarence Thomas, William Rehnquist, Kennedy, and Scalia dissenting. O'Connor, who authored the opinion described it as a "statutory weapon against behavior so severe that it impairs a victim's ability to learn."

The Real World?

The dissenters quickly labeled the decision an overreaction and overkill and it is instructive to look at Kennedy's immediate response to the majority opinion: "The real world of classroom discipline is a rough-and-tumble place where students practice newly learned vulgarities, erupt with anger, tease and embarrass each other, share offensive notes, flirt, push and shove in halls, grab and offend." This is the "schools never change" theory conflated with the more traditional "boys will be boys" adage. But notice that Kennedy doesn't mention "boys"—in his fantasy "rough-and-tumble" world. It is "students" who tease, push, erupt in anger, and shove. Well, chances are it is not girls who are "shoving" boys, and not gay kids and the geeks who are "teasing" and "pushing" the jocks. By removing the notion of social and physical power from the discussion Kennedy paints a portrait closer to *Andy Hardy's High School Romance* than the reality of high school violence—incipient, actual, and provoked. In his dissent Kennedy noted that the majority decision would "teach little Johnny a perverse lesson in Federalism." O'Connor quickly retorted that it simply "assures that Little Mary may attend class."

But *Davis v. Monroe County Board of Education* is no panacea and the majority opinion made clear that this was not to be used lightly; schools have to be proven to have done absolutely nothing to prevent "severe and persistent" sexual harassment. This means that if a harasser is sent to the principal's office or reprimanded even once the school may not be liable. The decision is also unclear on the parameters of sexual harassment and most probably would not cover anti-gay harassment (same-sex or not) unless it takes the specific form of sexual harassment. This means that a boy who is constantly called "faggot" would have no recourse under the law, but he might if he were taunted with "I'm gonna fuck you faggot."

Of course, either of these scenarios—neither unusual in many schools—are completely unacceptable and, if "severe" enough might even be covered on existing battery laws, but for the most part they are ignored by school authorities and teachers.

Violence Against Gay Students

Another aspect of the Littleton story that keeps surfacing (but is never fully articulated) is the rumor that Eric Harris and Dylan Klebold were gay. Their friends claim that this was not the case, but that—like many outsiders in high school hallways and gyms—they were taunted with the epithets of "fag," "homo," and "queer." The rumors that Harris and Klebold were homosexuals (not just the recipient of fag-geek name calling) were first spread by some Columbine students after the shooting. They have since been actively promoted by right-wing Christian spokespeople such as Reverend Fred Phelps and Reverend Jerry Falwell. While this is more cheap rhetoric for their ongoing anti-gay campaigns, the charge touches on a connection with one of the least discussed issues of school violence—that is students who are gay, or perceived to be gay, are likely to be targeted by this behavior.

In a Gallop poll 58 percent affirmed that "violence-prone" groups could be dangerous to gay students, with 50 percent reporting to have heard these groups espouse "hatred of gays." Fifty-one percent of the students also stated that "violence-prone" groups could be dangerous to black, Latino, or other minority students. Kevin Jennings, the executive director of Gay, Lesbian and Straight Education Network (GLSEN) notes "The anti-gay attitudes expressed in this study are not surprising—certainly not to us and probably not to the students who were polled. We can no longer afford to be surprised, or to lose these lessons on the very people responsible for keeping our students safe. There's simply no such thing as being a little safe. Either every student is safe or there's no meaningful safety at all."

THE AVAILABILITY OF GUNS AND SCHOOL VIOLENCE

Jann S. Wenner

Jann S. Wenner is the editor and publisher of *Rolling Stone*. In the following selection, he argues that school violence is undeniably linked to the wide availability of guns in America. Although political officials have deflected the debate on the causes of teenage violence away from guns and onto violent pop culture, Wenner points out, violent video games and movies—though they may be distasteful—are not the reason young people commit murder. The pop culture of many Western nations, such as Japan, is much more violent than that of the United States, but Japan's murder rate is lower because their citizens do not have easy access to guns, Wenner writes. According to Wenner, the only way to prevent further bloodshed in America's schools is to enact severely restrictive gun-control legislation.

The April 1999 massacre at Columbine High School in Littleton, Colorado, leaves us heartsick and outraged, not only because of the number of innocent children slain but also because this evil has taken place in the heart of the American dream. As much as we demand that tragedy teach us lessons, it is unlikely that we will learn how to devise a set of controls that can stop violence like this in the future.

But there is one blindingly obvious lesson: The nature and extent and devastation of the violence were directly and undeniably linked to the kind of weaponry that we have made widely available in America.

Nonetheless, we are going to hear a debate about the so-called causes of teenage violence. What are we going to get from this? Are we in the middle of some "national soul-searching," as President Clinton is trying to position it? Or are we going to get some amped-up rush to judgment and blame, driven by the voices of hysteria that generally drown out the more nuanced and understanding thinkers, who are less bloodthirsty in their political appetites and ambitions?

Will a modern McCarthyism take root in our high schools? Will any kid who is a bit too odd or angry now be viewed with suspicion? Are we going to "profile" children who dress in black, behave like outsiders, appear to be interested in violent movies or songs or officially disapproved video games? Shall we make the geeks even more isolated and humiliated?

Easy Access

We are likely going to get mired in the big muddy of a rhetorical, inconclusive debate about the "culture of violence." Do we really need a White House conference if it serves little purpose but to distract us from facing the real issue—which is that virtually every man, woman and child in the United States has easy access, day or night, to combat weapons and handguns?

We have to accept the reality that violence is part of the human condition and sometimes snaps in inexplicable and chaotic ways, and that despite this, the United States—alone among Western industrial societies—lets its population have open access to guns.

The cause, in the case of Littleton, will never be learned. Something went terribly wrong with two children, and their parents were powerless in the face of it. It was evil, and like all evil, great and small, it is a mystery. There are some things to which there are no answers.

In 1954, just as the baby boom began to enter its preteen years, in those last moments before the days of rock and roll, we had Senate hearings on juvenile delinquency that launched a crusade against horror and crime comic books, and ultimately led to their demise. Next, in the late Fifties and early Sixties, came the assaults on rock and roll—the attempts to censor it for its sexual suggestiveness, to blame it for youth riots and juvenile delinquency (again). FBI agents spent more than two years analyzing the lyrics to the hit single "Louie Louie" for a subliminal challenge to authority. In the 1980s, teenage violence was associated with rap or heavy-metal bands like Judas Priest, who were taken to court in Nevada in 1986 for their "subliminal" lyrics.

Pop Culture Is Not to Blame

But we're going to let rock and roll off the hook this time. No one, not even the most opportunistic culture warriors, believes that this attack has any political legs; rock is too popular to blame. The anti-Marilyn Manson crusade came to a silent halt within days of the Littleton massacre (though Manson has wisely taken himself off the concert circuit for the time being, showing a level of discretion and sensitivity that the National Rifle Association has refused to exercise).

So can we blame it on [director] Oliver Stone or *The Basketball Diaries*? We may find *Natural Born Killers* distasteful—I thought it artless, gratuitous violence but this approach is not likely to fly. . . . The most singularly violent movie of the last few years is Steven Spielberg's *Saving Private Ryan*, which raised the level of gore to stunning new heights. No one is going to argue that one, and no one is going to take on Spielberg, who is, after all, the establishment's favorite movie maker.

Movies and music will be safe; they are near universal, they've been around too long, and they are two of America's great cultural gifts to the world. So if we want to deal with the boogeyman instead of the guns, what do we have left? Video games—violent video games—are going to be the new demon for liberals and conservatives alike. They are going to take a whipping worse than horror comics or rock and roll ever did.

There is some genuinely unpleasant stuff out there: blood and guts, severed spinal cords, a technological hierarchy of violence—gore and weapons as cool and as real as what those Apache [helicopter] pilots see in their visor screens. And these games are complex and multidimensional, with symbolism worthy of Dante.

Easy Answers

They are going to be a bonanza for psychologists, sociologists, legitimate experts of every stripe and discipline. The police will weigh in, and military-training experts will talk about the games' similarities to the programs used to train infantry for high-kill rates, as if schoolkids and professional soldiers are the same.

Indeed, because we find some of these games distasteful and unfamiliar, we are going to fear them. And we are going to find them easy for us to blame and easy for us to attack, and we will all congratulate ourselves that in so doing we have been able to do something. And it will be *easy*; we will be glad to see this stuff go.

The powerful men who control the multibillion-dollar television, music and movie empires are surely preparing themselves now to defend their profits and their freedoms, and our rights to free and creative expression, no matter how offensive it sometimes may seem. But they should not make the mistake of failing to defend those rights for the creators of video games. They cannot afford to jettison them; if they do, they jeopardize themselves morally, and they invite us to impugn their motives—because, after all, video games are clear competitive threats to their share of the youthful entertainment dollar.

Fantasy vs. Reality

It's possible that such games *might* reinforce the feelings of isolation and anger of psychologically distressed children, but there is no convincing proof that the games are a cause of their initial vulnerability or that they are a trigger mechanism. Children, because they play violent fantasy games, do not then go on to murder their classmates.

Adolescents are fully capable of distinguishing fantasy violence—whether in music, movies or video games—from real violence. Apparently the grownups in Washington are not.

Students, when they arrive in their classrooms, want to know not whether their schoolmates have been playing video games but whether they are carrying guns.

It is useless to blame the parents of Eric Harris and Dylan Klebold—as useless as it is to blame the parents of the young killers in Pearl, Mississippi; West Paducah, Kentucky; Jonesboro, Arkansas; and Springfield, Oregon. From what we know of them, they were caring parents who spent time with their kids and were active in the community. But in each case, they lived in states with lax gun-control laws and had easy access to guns.

The Availability of Guns

There are 192 million privately owned firearms in the United States, with 7.5 million guns being added to that total each year. In a recent *Rolling Stone*/MTV poll of twelve- to twenty-four-year-olds (taken five days before the Columbine shootings), eighty-four percent of them said they had easy access to firearms.

A parent is not able to stop this open commerce in guns. A parent does not possess the ability to design and manufacture a kid-proof gun or mandate the use of the latest fingerprint-recognition technology. Only governments can do this.

In Japan, Canada, Australia and, indeed, most Western industrialized nations, violent movies, music and video games are the norm, but access to firearms is not. In 1996, handguns were used to murder 2 people in New Zealand, 15 in Japan, 30 in Great Britain, 106 in Canada, 213 in Germany and 9,390 in the United States.

According to the Centers for Disease Control, more American children are killed by firearms than by all natural causes combined.

It is clear that it's now the responsibility of the community and society to provide more proactive forms of support for parents. Even the most responsible, trained gun owner, with safety locks on his weapons, is powerless. It's not the Fifties—Mom's not home all day, monitoring the kids; she's at work. We need to begin creating a nearly gun-free society and thoughtful community safety nets for adolescents. In the phrase of Hillary Clinton, it takes a village to raise a child.

It Is Time for Tough Legislation

The performance of President Clinton in the aftermath of the Columbine killings has been discouraging. The entertainment industry makes an easy, feel-good target, but in the end there is no clear, plausible relationship between entertainment and violent behavior—unlike the distinct relationship between Eric Harris' TEC-9 semiautomatic pistol and some of the fifteen dead in Colorado.

"President Clinton should seize the moment," the *Washington Post* wrote in its April 26, 1999, lead editorial, "to do more than offer photo-op hand wringings in classrooms or endorsements of constructive but piecemeal approaches to the terror of gunfire. He should stand up for a national ban on the general sale, manufacture and ownership of handguns."

It is time for the president to call for tough, severely restrictive gun-control legislation that begins the process of diminishing the massive arsenal that tears away at our social fabric and our families. It is time to go way beyond ineffective measures like the so-called assault-weapons ban, which is so riddled with loopholes that these guns are still legally and freely available to an eighteen-year-old boy with a grudge.

Instead, Clinton offers to "bury the hatchet" with the NRA and asks its leaders to sit beside media executives in the search for solutions to violence. This is ridiculous. The hunters and sportsmen with whom we might reason do not control the NRA; its fanatic leadership cannot be replaced by a majority vote of the membership, since the bylaws appear to have been blatantly rigged in favor of a small minority, a situation that warrants investigation.

Gun Fanaticism

The NRA has to be taken on directly and unequivocally; nearly eighty percent of Americans favor tough, restrictive laws. That majority has been frustrated not only by the NRA's ruthless use of money and fanaticism, but also by the lack of effective leadership from the gun-control movement and by President Clinton's failure to commit to this issue as anything much more than a public-relations exercise.

There is no making nice here; these are not nice people. Charlton Heston is unblinking in the face of the images of students fleeing Columbine High School. "Our mission is to remain a steady beacon of strength for the Second Amendment, even if it has no other friends on the planet," he said. "We cannot let tragedy lay waste to the most rare and hard-won human right in history."

The Second Amendment does *not*, in fact, guarantee to citizens the absolute right to bear arms. In 1992, six former attorneys general, Democratic and Republican, signed a statement that said, "For more than 200 years, the federal courts have unanimously determined that the Second Amendment concerns only the arming of the people in service to an organized state militia; it does not guarantee immediate access to guns for private purposes. The nation can no longer afford to let the gun lobby's distortion of the Constitution cripple every reasonable attempt to implement an effective national policy toward guns and crime."

Take Away the Real Guns

It is patent insanity to think that art causes violence. Music doesn't put guns in the hands of children. Video games are not the root cause of teenage anger. Art—high or low—is not the culprit. You don't stop children from hurting other children by stopping them from playing with toy guns , which is essentially what violent video games are. You protect children by taking away real guns.

Does anyone really think we're going to live in a safer society if we don't have video games, if children can't play Dungeons and Dragons? Are we a better society if we demand that musicians and filmmakers and game designers not portray violence? It's not culture that created the killing fields in Springfield, Oregon; in Jonesboro, Arkansas; in West Paducah, Kentucky; in Pearl, Mississippi; in Littleton, Colorado; or in the place where this happens next; it's the guns.

THE INDIVIDUALS WITH DISABILITIES EDUCATION ACT CONTRIBUTES TO VIOLENCE IN SCHOOLS

William J. Cahir

The Individuals with Disabilities Education Act (IDEA) prevents school officials from disciplining and expelling disabled students with behavior problems, contends William J. Cahir, senior reporter for *Education Daily*. Even if a disabled student commits a serious infraction of the rules, such as bringing a gun to school, he or she can only be suspended for ten days, as opposed to the mandatory one-year expulsion handed to other students accused of the same crime, Cahir relates. He points out that some school officials and politicians are seeking to modify IDEA, to make it easier to remove disruptive students with emotional and behavioral disorders from the classroom. However, many lawmakers are hesitant to implement such changes because they do not want to risk angering disability interest groups, writes Cahir.

Benny Gooden, superintendent of schools in Fort Smith, Arkansas, remembers the 1996 incident well. Four youths were involved. One sold the .345 pistol, another bought it, a third hid it in his locker. And the fourth—a student with a disability—stole it.

Gooden expelled the first three for a full academic year. But he suspended the disabled student, provided a tutor at the boy's home, and subsequently returned the boy to his previous educational placement in school. Parents were furious.

"That doesn't play well down at the Rotary Club," Gooden said. "Taxpayers do not understand that. They don't think that's justice."

Gooden wasn't indulging the disabled student. He was complying with the nation's main special education law, the Individuals with Disabilities Education Act (IDEA).

IDEA requires public schools to provide physically, mentally, and emotionally challenged children with equal educational opportunities. To prevent schools from routinely expelling disabled kids with behavior problems, IDEA curtails administrators' ability to punish

Excerpted from "Does the Federal Special Education Law Contribute to Violence in Schools?" by William J. Cahir, *The New Democrat*, May/June 1999.

them—including those who might be psychologically disturbed but otherwise blend into the student body.

A Dangerous Catch-22

The recent spate of mass murders in public schools has kept school safety high atop the national agenda. As this magazine went to press, it was not known whether the two teenagers who killed 12 classmates, a teacher, and themselves in April 1999 at Columbine High School in Littleton, Colorado, were special education students; federal law forbids public disclosure of student records. According to media reports, one of the shooters, Eric Harris, had agreed to undergo a mental health evaluation and had been prescribed an anti-depressant drug as part of a plea bargain in 1998 on charges of breaking into a car along with the other shooter, Dylan Klebold.

If the young men who committed the Littleton murders were in fact deemed disabled, they would have been eligible for treatment that could have prevented their bloody rampage. On the other hand, if they were special education students, they also would have been protected against routine punishment for serious misbehavior by the federal law's heightened due-process standards.

Many school officials argue that IDEA creates a dangerous Catch-22: If a student's violent or antisocial behavior stems from a disability, the officials' disciplinary options become limited. Only when a child's education team determines that his misconduct is unrelated to his disability may the school discipline the student as it would others.

IDEA generally lets educators suspend a disabled child for no more than 10 school days. Disabled students charged with weapons and drug-related offenses can be removed from their school and sent to an alternative placement for a maximum of 45 calendar days. (In contrast, the 1994 federal Gun-Free Schools Act *requires* that any non-disabled child who possesses a gun in school be expelled for at least one year.) Schools also can move a disabled student to an alternative placement if a hearing officer determines the student poses a threat to himself or others—a litigious, appealable, time-consuming process.

Dual National Discipline Code

In the eyes of the nation's school superintendents, IDEA has created a dual national discipline code, mandating one set of rules for disabled students and another for everyone else.

David Wolk, superintendent of schools in Rutland, Vermont, wants Congress to modify IDEA so that children with emotional and behavioral disorders can be more easily removed from regular classes. He has discussed the idea with Senator James Jeffords, chairman of the Senate Health, Education, Labor, and Pensions Committee.

"If a student poses a threat, regardless of any individualized differences, then that student should be removed from the educational setting," Wolk says.

John Jordon, superintendent in Oxford, Mississippi, and an adviser to Senate Majority Leader Trent Lott, says Congress could simplify IDEA by creating a separate discipline policy for students with learning disabilities. "We're not talking about kids with autism," he says, explaining that they are not the discipline problem. "We are talking about specific learning-disabled children."

Educators complain that discipline problems are rampant in schools today, with offenses ranging from cursing to sexual harassment, from fighting to assault. Not surprisingly, school administrators' complaints about IDEA have caught the attention of Congress. Lawmakers have introduced three bills to repeal IDEA's due-process standards and let schools punish students with and without disabilities in the same manner.

Lawmakers concerned about the nexus between special education and school discipline are treading lightly, however, for fear of incurring the wrath of disability interest groups.

IDEA discipline policy is only part of the debate, says Delaine Eastin, chief of public instruction in California. "People are a lot more concerned about the lack of special education funding overall than they are about this issue."

The Littleton massacre is certain to raise the profile of school safety and discipline in Congress, which is slated to reauthorize both the Elementary and Secondary Education Act and the Juvenile Justice and Delinquency Prevention Act in 1999. President Clinton has called on schools to adopt "sensible" discipline policies. Republicans, meanwhile, have introduced bills that would require states to prosecute children ages 14 and older as adults for crimes committed at school or anywhere else.

School safety has already worked its way into the 2000 presidential campaign. Republican candidate Lamar Alexander, for example, argues in a television spot that "it's time to put discipline back in the classrooms and get the troublemakers out."

"Give teachers clear authority to remove disruptive students," says Alexander, the education secretary under George Bush. "Support teachers who maintain discipline instead of suing them."

Criticism of the Hard-Line Approach

Some academics warn that the hard-line approach Alexander favors holds little promise of curtailing school violence. According to Jeffrey Sprague, co-director of the University of Oregon's Institute on Violence and Destructive Behavior, research suggests that schools using punishment, including expulsion and suspension, as their primary discipline tools have higher rates of student aggression, vandalism, and truancy. Sprague advises schools to adopt clear punishment policies, teach expected standards of conduct to children, and enforce rules consistently. Students learn what to expect, he contends, and erupt less frequently.

Kevin Dwyer, president of the National Association of School Psychologists, begs lawmakers and school administrators to resist the temptation to expel all troublesome children.

"We're neglecting children," Dwyer says. "That's why we're ending up with all this violence and kids being impulsive and difficult to deal with in school. . . . It's overwhelming out there, the lack of services for kids."

Other educators raise a more hard-boiled objection to kicking violent or unruly students out of school. "The smart people, including fairly conservative school leaders, are saying you don't want [kids] out there on the street," says California's Eastin.

Chicago has adopted a citywide discipline code for its 559 schools. Any student who gets into a fistfight can expect to participate in a parent conference and get a three-day suspension.

"It's most important to us that we have a structure, that everyone can understand 'here's what to expect,'" explains Cozette Buckney, chief education officer for the Chicago system.

The school district modified its zero-tolerance policy for guns and drugs in 1997 to include offenses committed off school grounds. So a Chicago student arrested on a Friday night for possessing drugs can count on disciplinary action when he returns to school on Monday.

New York State United Teachers (NYSUT), the state affiliate of the American Federation of Teachers, recently surveyed 605 of its members on school safety issues. Forty percent said they had either been attacked by, broken up fights among, or otherwise had physical confrontations with students during the past three years. Sixty percent said students' profanity and defiance were problems in class, and 66 percent said they wanted parents to be better disciplinarians.

"Many students who are chronically disruptive or violent are on the fast track to even bigger trouble," says Antonia Cortese, NYSUT's first vice president. "With good alternative programs, we can turn a lot of these kids around." The union has asked the state to empower its members to eject misbehaving students from their classes and send them to new state-financed alternative schools.

Results in Texas

Texas is one of only seven states to give teachers such wide discretion. Backers of the state's 1995 Safe Schools Act say it has reduced the incidence of verbal abuse, threats, vandalism, assault, and other serious offenses in schools. "Now the teacher has the right to keep these hooligans who don't care if they disrupt the learning environment from doing that," says John Cole, president of the Texas Federation of Teachers. "If the only thing we accomplish is getting these kids out of the class so others can learn, then that's worthwhile."

In April 1998, Senators John Kerry and Gordon Smith introduced a bill that would give school districts federal grants to open alternative schools, crisis centers, and in-school suspension rooms. But this problem-solving approach runs against the current tide in Congress, which is to consolidate rather than create federal education programs.

Alternative placements for antisocial students are an imperfect solution. Many students who return to their home schools from such centers slip back into bad social and academic patterns. Long-term placements are just as problematic; few of the programs help troubled youths make the transition to employment or higher education. But educators say such specialized schools do have one crucial advantage: They isolate dangerous children from teachers, school staff, and other students.

According to Carol Kochar of the University of Oregon violence institute, the best alternative programs share one characteristic: "the presence of caring, dedicated adults." Clearly, if we as a nation decide to begin segregating more and more "problem children" in their own schools, we are going to have to find more money to fund those schools and a new generation of highly trained instructors and counselors to staff them.

LIBERALISM IS RESPONSIBLE FOR THE SCHOOL MASSACRE IN LITTLETON

Samuel Francis

The media coverage of the 1999 shootings at Columbine High School in Littleton, Colorado, has been plagued with inaccuracies, writes syndicated columnist Samuel Francis. According to Francis, the major news agencies and many politicians quickly characterized teenage gunmen Eric Harris and Dylan Klebold as racist neo-Nazis. However, later discoveries made it clear that Harris and Klebold were not motivated by right-wing fanaticism and instead had grown up in liberal homes. Human nature, the propensity that all human beings have to explode, is what inspired the Littleton gunmen, Francis maintains. Because liberal philosophy tries to mask the truth about human nature and human society, it is also to blame for the deaths at Columbine, the author concludes.

"When I think back on all the crap I learned in high school . . . ," Paul Simon mused in a popular song some years ago. Simon, of course, was in high school long before multiculturalism, Afrocentrism, Outcome-Based Education, bilingual education, Heather Has 17 Mommies, Holocaust Studies, and assorted therapeutic group gropes and mass séances in "counseling" displaced the deathless vapidities about history, life, and literature that typically spill from the lips of teachers in all ages and nations. But no matter what sort of crap Simon endured in his high school and what sort poisons the minds and spirits of teenagers today, it is nothing compared to the offal that the American news media regularly inject into grown-ups and anyone else who pays attention to them.

Inaccurate Reporting

The mass murder of 12 students at Littleton, Colorado's Columbine High School on April 20, 1999, was the occasion for the construction of a veritable mountain of journalistic chicken doodle by almost every major newspaper and news service in the world. The blood had not stopped flowing before the ace reporters and investigative jour-

Excerpted from "I Was a Teenage Werewolf," by Samuel Francis, *Chronicles: A Magazine of American Culture,* August 1999. Reprinted with permission from *Chronicles: A Magazine of American Culture,* a publication of The Rockford Institute, 928 N. Main St., Rockford, IL 61103.

nalists had the whole gory mess all figured out and ready to serve, hot and piping, to a gape-jawed public. As it turned out, almost everything they reported was wrong—some of it almost certainly deliberately wrong—and not only wrong, but a carefully crafted wrongness that pointed in the exact opposite direction of the truth about Littleton and a lot of other things in the United States that it is important for some people to hide.

The two teenage killers, Eric Harris and Dylan Klebold, an Associated Press story told us on April 21, 1999, were "said to be part of an outcast group with right-wing overtones called the Trenchcoat Mafia." "Students said the group was fascinated with World War II and the Nazis and noted that Tuesday [April 20] was Adolf Hitler's birthday," it continued. The same day, yet another AP story described the "Trenchcoat Mafia" as a group that "hated blacks, Hispanics, Jews and athletes." A student named Aaron Cohn, repeatedly quoted in several stories, claimed the "Mafia" "often made anti-Semitic comments"; he was the apparent source of the story that the killers had called the black student they murdered by a racial epithet, while other students said the group or the killers themselves wore "Nazi crosses" and "made generally derogatory remarks about Hispanics and blacks." "They talked about Hitler and wore clothes with German insignia," gasped the *New York Times* on April 23, 1999. "They hated jocks, admired Nazis and scorned normalcy. . . . They were white supremacists . . . ," the *Washington Post* bubbled the same day.

And so it went for the next week or so, with proponents of more gun control, more voodoo education, more hate-crime laws, and more federal manipulation of schools, law enforcement, and families flapping their wings and their jaws overtime, intent on squeezing every possible ounce of political advantage from what the press at once dubbed "the worst attack on a school in American history." Even that wasn't true. In 1927, a school board member named Andrew Kehos planted several dynamite bombs under his local schoolhouse in Michigan and blew it to splinters, killing himself and 45 other people, including 38 students. Whether Mr. Kehos was also reported to have "right-wing overtones" and to be a "white supremacist" is not known, but that atrocity committed by a lunatic, like most others in civilized countries, was soon forgotten.

Media Exploitation

The Littleton massacre wasn't forgotten, at least not for several weeks after it happened, and it soon became clear that the media were trying to use it in almost exactly the same way they had exploited the Oklahoma City bombing of April 19, 1995. They were setting a Reichstag fire, creating a vast and elaborate lie that sought to pin the blame for the Littleton massacre on "the right."

But the Littleton Lie couldn't last because it was just so contrary to certain facts that soon began to emerge from the carnage, and in any case, the Lie was largely irrelevant to the main political usage of the massacre, more gun control. Yet the major media kept the Littleton incident on their front pages for at least two weeks after it occurred; it was only when the facts did emerge that they lost interest in it and the story began to follow Mr. Kehos and his dynamite bombs into that subcontinent of oblivion reserved for inconvenient facts and truths. The facts, you see, not only gave the lie to the Littleton Lie but pointed to a truth the news media didn't want to bring up.

One glimpse of reality began to creep onto the national screen when the contents of Eric Harris's website were released. Those contents had been reported to the local police by an alarmed parent more than a year before young Master Harris tripped over the edge on April 20, 1999, but the cops had ignored them. As soon as the massacre occurred, however, America Online shut down the Harris website, and no one got a gander at what was on it until the *New York Times,* to its credit, reported at least some of the contents on May 1, 1999.

The Contents of the Harris Website

The *Times* found the following passage, written by Harris, "intriguing": "You know what I hate?" Harris "repeatedly asked readers of the site," the *Times* reported. "One of the answers he gave was, 'RACISM!'" "He wrote that people who are biased against 'blacks, Asians, Mexicans or people from any other country or race besides white-American' should 'have their arms ripped off' and be burned." "'Don't let me catch you making fun of someone just because they are of a different color,' he wrote." Young Master Harris, it turns out, hated many things besides "RACISM," among them fans of *Star Wars,* people who mispronounce words, liars, country music, freedom of expression, opponents of the death penalty, and smokers. But "RACISM," so far from being a creed to which he subscribed, was definitely on the enemies list.

As for Dylan Klebold, it soon came out that he was of Jewish background and that his grandfather had been a prominent Jewish philanthropist in Ohio. In fact, young Master Klebold was reported to have taken part in a Passover seder only shortly before the massacre. Whatever motivated him to splatter the schoolhouse with the brains of his pals, it probably wasn't the admiration for Hitler and the Nazis that the press had attributed to him and his colleague, nor did Eric Harris's website reveal any sympathy for Hitler or for "racism" or indeed for any "right-wing overtones" except perhaps his enthusiasm for capital punishment.

But what finally and definitely exposed the fantasies, speculations, unexamined assumptions, and outright lies the news media concocted and inflicted on us for two weeks was an interview in the *New York Times* on April 30, 1999, with several students at the high school who had actually known the killers. What they had to say should have ended the professional careers of several of the con artists who pass themselves off as "reporters" and whose misreporting had already fabricated myths and legends about the Littleton killings that will probably never die completely.

The infamous "Trenchcoat Mafia" that was supposedly behind the bloodshed, said 16-year-old Devon Adams, consisted of about 15 or 20 people who wore black trenchcoats as a kind of clique uniform. They played cards and hung out and smoked together. "That's all it was," and anyway, more than half of them had graduated in 1998; the group barely existed anymore. Harris and Klebold weren't even part of it, he told the *Times*.

Obsessed with Hitler?

Well, but what about the racism, the sympathy for Hitler, the obsession with World War II? Meg Hains, 17, said,

> I am black/white mixed. And when the media is coming up with this thing that Dylan and Eric were racist they weren't. They were my friends. They were very nice to me, both of them. I don't get this whole racial thing that people are coming up with.

Miss Hains, you can see, has a lot to learn, and no doubt a good deal of the remainder of her learning experience will be devoted to "getting" the "whole racial thing" with which her elders are so obsessed. Devon Adams acknowledged that Harris and Klebold did use "racial slurs," but "I don't think it meant that they were racist." "What about the Nazi stuff?" the *Times* insisted. Meg Hains replied, "That is the biggest load of [expletive] I've ever heard. They never wore swastikas around their arm[s]. Never. Not in this entire year that I've known them. No." Devon Adams said, "They're not Nazis. They didn't worship Nazis." They read books about Nazis because they were studying World War II history in school, he said. The report that they shouted "Heil Hitler" when bowling was also untrue, said Dustin Thurman, 18. . . .

In short, when the press told the public that Harris and Klebold were "white supremacists," "right-wingers," "racists," "neo-Nazis," etc., they lied. Journalists assumed, probably because unconsciously they have come to believe their own propaganda line, that all mass violence is the work of the "right," a catch-all term that can include anyone from Elizabeth Dole to the Aryan Nations. If it's the assassination of a president, the bombing of a federal building, or the mass murder of high-school students by wigged-out teenagers full of pubescent resentment, plugged-up hormones, and the mental and moral garbage regularly served them by their schools, their televisions, their movies, their music, their books, their government and their newspapers, then it has to be because "the right" is on the march. And of course, this myth is useful for discrediting anyone who really is on "the right" when he questions the quack nostrums and increased state power that the left demands as a "solution" to the "crisis."

Human Nature Was Responsible for Littleton

What, then, did cause the massacre at Littleton? The simple answer is "human nature," the propensity that all human beings have to explode, as Mr. Kehos exploded back in 1927 and as lots of other people do in one way or another every now and then. Of course, not everybody does explode. Why did Eric Harris and Dylan Klebold do so?

The question is probably still unanswerable, but one story that popped up in the *Washington Post* is suggestive. A woman who was a friend of the Klebold family recalls that Dylan used to play with her daughters and remembers telling his mother that in her house she had only girl toys while in your house, you have only "boy toys." "Boy toys," replied Mrs. Klebold, "but no toy guns."

Dylan Klebold's father is said to be "a liberal who favors gun control," yet another Associated Press story reported several days after the killings. His mother worked in a community program that helped "disabled students gain access to education." When Dylan and Eric broke into a car and got caught, they were placed in an "anger management" program, and the police who ran the program praised them for their conduct. As for Mark Manes, the pal of Eric and Dylan who sold them the semi-automatic pistol they used in the shootings, his mother is a member of Handgun Control, Inc., the country's largest gun-control lobbying organization. "She has been against guns forever," Manes' lawyer told the *New York Times*. "Mark grew up in a house where no weapons were present." Much the same seems to have been true of Eric Harris, who was an enthusiastic fan of Bill Clinton's bombing of Serbia. "I hope we do go to war," he told a classmate. "I'll be the first one there." That's exactly why Harris tried to enlist in the Marines a few days before the blow-up at school. Maybe it wasn't Marilyn Manson that lit his fuse so much as the *Weekly Standard* or the *Wall Street Journal* editorial page.

Liberal Lies

The dirty little truth the American propaganda machine won't tell us directly, the secret that has to be pried out from between the lines of the machine's unreliable newspapers and thinly disguised politicization, is that all three of these young men grew up in the make-believe world concocted by liberalism, a fantastic place where race and sex mean nothing; where violence and crime don't exist and guns have no function and no meaning, even as toys; where wars against "ethnic nationalists" for "humanitarian goals" are morally imperative but owning a handgun to protect your home and family ought to be a crime; where war is only one more goody-good community project like getting disabled students access to education; where people who adhere to "RACISM!" deserve to have their arms ripped off and be burned, and human beings, including healthy young men whose genes and glands and brains drive them to aggression and conflict, are simply blank slates to be shaped and twisted and scribbled over by "anger management" programs and all the therapeutic witchcraft that Hillary Clinton and her friends really believe in. It was not Adolf Hitler or Marilyn Manson or guns or the "right" that made Eric Harris and Dylan Klebold pop their corks in April 1999 but liberalism itself and all the illusions liberalism conjures up to mask the truths about human beings and human society that it refuses to face. That's a secret the news media can't expose, partly because those who run them can't even recognize it and partly because, if they ever did, the whole system constructed on the lies of liberalism would crumble.

CHAPTER 3

SCHOOL VIOLENCE: PERSONAL NARRATIVES

Survivors Discuss School Violence

New York Times

On April 20, 1999, Eric Harris and Dylan Klebold shot and killed twelve of their classmates and one teacher before killing themselves at Columbine High School in Littleton, Colorado. In the following selection, originally published days after the massacre, the *New York Times* interviews eight students from Columbine: sixteen-year-old sophomore Devon Adams, sixteen-year-old sophomore Jessica Cave, sixteen-year-old sophomore Richard Colbert, seventeen-year-old junior Andrew Fraser, seventeen-year-old junior Meg Hains, eighteen-year-old senior Nick Jackson, eighteen-year-old senior Jeni LaPlante, and eighteen-year-old senior Dustin Thurman. The students discuss their views on high school cliques, violent pop culture, and how the mass shooting in their school has affected their lives.

Before the gunshots rang out in fifth period at Columbine High School on April 20, 1999, students there were busy with the everyday life of American teen-agers. Now, after a massacre that took 15 lives, including those of the two classmates who were the gunmen, the students wonder where they and their school go on from here.

Across the country, the mass shooting again raised questions about teen-agers and the often violent popular culture they are immersed in. What did the assault say about growing up today, the pressures of high school, the fragility of teen-age identity? Did it say anything at all?

In an effort to find answers, the *New York Times* invited eight Columbine students—four young women and four young men—to talk about the violence in their school and how it has changed the way they look at the world.

Their nearly two-hour discussion touched on cliques, guns, race, music, video games and fashion—and the nightmares that now keep some of them from sleeping. The main themes have been distilled from a transcript for this article.

New York Times: Tell us about the trench coat mafia.

Devon Adams: Last year the trench coat mafia consisted of 15 to 20 people. They were a group of kids who maybe played Magic, that card game, and went out and smoked together. That's all it was. And, yes, they happened to wear black trench coats. They called themselves the trench coat mafia.

It fell apart because half those people graduated last year. You hear all this talk, about the trench coat mafia, whatever—Dylan and Eric weren't even a part of that, first off. I just want everybody to know the trench coat mafia is just another name, just another way to place blame. Because those people who were in the trench coat mafia or whatever, aren't even part of it anymore.

New York Times: We've heard a lot about social cliques in Columbine. How powerful are they?

Adams: I don't think the cliques were really that intense. Lots and lots of people knew people from both groups. A lot of people are from both sides of the gun. I mean, they were friends with the trench coat mafia and then they were friends with the, you know, the jocks or whatever you want to call them.

Jeni LaPlante: I don't think it was really cliques. It's more like groups of friends. I was talking a couple months back with the class president, Heather, and we were saying how much it's changed since eighth grade, where you had the distinct groups. Once you're a senior, you know, everyone is just—we thought everyone was friends.

I guess we weren't, but—it was more like groups of friends, not, you know, we don't talk to them and we're going to raise our noses at them.

Nick Jackson: I think our school is such a great place. If you played a sport, or whatever you did, it was such a great place to go. And I don't think we should be remembered for what happened that day, but for how great we were. I want my brother to go to school there, wrestle there, and graduate from Columbine. It's just such a great school that it can't end in such a tragedy.

New York Times: How do sports affect social groupings?

Jackson: It wasn't like just the jocks hung out with the jocks, to me. I hung out with everybody. And I wasn't mean to people who didn't play a sport. I didn't think any less of somebody who didn't.

New York Times: Did some athletes?

Jackson: Yeah, there were some.

LaPlante: It was a lot worse last year.

New York Times: In what ways?

LaPlante: Just with big jocks picking on little jocks, or big jocks picking on, you know, skaters.

New York Times: Who are you talking about? What groups?

Dustin Thurman: Football players, mostly.

Pride and Respect

New York Times: Nick, you're a wrestler. What's it like to be an athlete at Columbine?

Jackson: On the day before a meet, we wear our warm-ups, and we wear them with pride. It just feels so good to walk around knowing that you're wearing a warm-up that says Columbine Rebels. It's just the impact of being a part of the school in whatever you do. It's a great thing.

Thurman: I think you've got maybe a little more respect if you played sports, or people look at you differently.

New York Times: How do people treat athletes?

Thurman: You don't ever get bad looks or anything.

Andrew Fraser: I think the other reason that they're sometimes treated with more respect is because there's a whole lot of school spirit at Columbine. People really stand up for their teams, and the athletes are the ones that actually perform the tasks and, you know, give the school some of its pride. They're the ones that give the school a sense of accomplishment.

Adams: I'm on the Columbine forensics team, speech and debate. We have some people who play football on our team, some people who are cheerleaders. But we have a problem with the athletes sometimes. At the prom assembly, when our national qualifiers went up and our state champion went up, there was booing. And I looked over and they were wearing football shirts.

It's really sad that that happens because I respect people who wrestle and play football, because I could never even do that. It's so sad that academics are so low on our ranking, because it's something else to be proud of. There needs to be school spirit for everything.

Thurman: I just had a question. What are considered jocks? Because there are so many sports in our school.

Jackson: I think every time I hear somebody call somebody a jock, I think it's the same as them calling me, like, an expletive or something like that. Because every time somebody calls somebody a jock it's in that kind of tone. You know, it's like, hey jock.

Meg Hains: Jock is a kind of slang down term, like some people will call other people freaks because their hair is different.

New York Times: Where did Eric Harris and Dylan Klebold fit in?

Adams: Dylan Klebold was one of my best friends. And when I hung out with him, there was just something that happened. I mean, whether they were wearing jeans and a T-shirt, or whether they were wearing their black trench coats, people would give them looks. Just like, "You don't belong here, would you leave?"

Let's block out last week when I say this—they hadn't done anything physically wrong to people. I mean, they dressed different. So? They wore black. So what? It's just, they were hated and so they felt they hated back. They hated back.

Hains: They'd call them freaks, weirdos, faggots. It was just stupid name calling, acting like little children. It's like my cousins come home, they're only 2 and 3, and they come home and start calling me names, calling each other names like butt-head and all these other things. They probably couldn't handle it.

Adams: People called them fags. People thought they were gay. And that's not right. I mean, even if they were—and which, they're not—it's not right to say that.

Thurman: When they call them fag, I think it's a slang term for, like, loser. I don't think they really meant that. They were like nerds.

"Going to Have Different Cliques"

Fraser: I believe these guys could have been taunted pretty easily, because there are many different people in our school that do this. But I want to speak not as a jock or an athlete, but for them, in saying that these are not the only type of people who should be targeted. It's just natural at any high school that you're going to have different cliques.

I can see how these guys could have easily caught a lot of, not always physical abuse, but just verbal—someone happening to walk by in the hall and saying, "Hey, buddy, nice lipstick," just small things that I think really built up over time. But it wasn't just one group or person in particular.

Hains: I have a friend, he doesn't dress like everybody else. He wears heavy metal band T-shirts, black shorts no matter what the weather, and a black hat, and he has long hair. And friends who normally just come up to me and talk to me and are so nice to me—when I'm around him, they give me looks. And people come up to me after I talk to him, they're like, "How can you talk to him? How can you even acknowledge his presence?" I'm like, "It's simple, he's nice."

That was the same with Eric and Dylan. I knew both of them. I went bowling with them occasionally. And they were extremely nice. They never showed any signs that they'd like to go off and hurt people.

Jackson: I don't think there's a lot of stereotyping. If I saw Eric walk by, I'd ignore him, I wouldn't go talk to him, because what would we talk about? We have no interests that are the same. I don't think he wants to go in the wrestling room and practice with me.

Thurman: Everyone says we stereotype them. But I think they stereotype themselves, too. Because I had both in class with me, and they would not talk to anyone. They acted like they had no spirit at all.

Doom Can Relieve Stress

New York Times: Adults are concerned about violent computer games and song lyrics. Is this a large part of teen-age life today?

Hains: I've played the game Doom that they're saying Dylan and Eric constantly played. And I don't think it was that game. I'd go to school and there were people that would so royally piss me off, and I'd just go home and I'd sit on that game for hours, just taking out my stress on it. And the next day I'd be perfectly fine.

That's the way I get rid of my stress, instead of going out and really killing people. It saves a lot of time. I know this sounds weird, but some violent games are a therapy for kids.

Jessica Cave: I think that works for some people. But for someone who gets teased and ridiculed and gets angry every day at people and then actually has things going through their mind like that—I think Marilyn Manson and games like that do influence them. I think it builds up even more.

And they wore black. I'm not saying that's bad, or stupid, I'm just saying that it is a very depressing color that they wore every day. And that sort of reflects on their attitudes toward things.

New York Times: What's the appeal of Marilyn Manson?

Jackson: Insane. Drugs.

Cave: Insanity, yeah. Craziness.

Adams: Okay, they listened to Marilyn Manson, but not like some people. They listened to him every once in a while. They listened to Nine Inch Nails. They listened to Rammstein.

They listened to Rammstein and Nine Inch Nails and KMFDM because of the beats. Because Dylan wanted to be a drummer. He didn't even know what they were saying in Rammstein. He doesn't speak German. He just liked the beat of the song. The same with Dr. Octagon, D.J. Spookie, all those techno bands. They've got these beats to them.

Cave: They may have listened to them for the beats, but after someone listens to that crap over and over and over for the beats, they do hear the lyrics and it is in their subconscious.

New York Times: What do the guys here think?

Thurman: I have most of those CD's that they're talking about. It doesn't bother me.

New York Times: Why do you like them?

Thurman: I don't really agree with the words that they're saying. But when I'm listening to it I can turn it up real loud and get out aggression while I'm, like, driving. And, I like the beats, like you said. But it's not making me psycho listening.

Richard Colbert: Everybody takes it differently, and you can make it into things that it's not. Like people blame music and video games and all these outside influences as scapegoats. And all the people on, like, *Dateline* that are doing this, they're like 50 years old. They don't know that stuff. They don't know what we're talking about.

Guns

New York Times: How do young people view guns?

Hains: I am utterly afraid of guns. When I heard somebody had a gun, I was fine, but then I had to jump over the pit fence and I couldn't make it. My arms just went totally wobbly. And then I found out he was shooting people. I broke down into tears, a mass of tears. I couldn't find my best friend. And this was all over guns.

Thurman: I have all my guns in my room in a case. I have bullets and everything.

New York Times: How many guns do you have?

Thurman: How many? Probably six or seven. I could run around and start shooting people easily. But it's morals. You just know right from wrong. My parents have trained me with guns and everything and my sister.

New York Times: Does anyone else have guns in the house?

Fraser: We have guns at our house. A lot of times it's owned by the parents for protection. But I have a lot of friends who, like Dustin said, have literally an arsenal of shotguns and high-powered rifles at their house. But he's right, it is about morals and when they are used. About self-control.

New York Times: All of these shootings have occurred at white middle-class schools. What do you make of that?

Fraser: Nothing in particular. Columbine is definitely white. I would say of the around 2,000 kids, there are at most 200 black kids. I'm not sure if I'm right on that.

General Comments: Not that many. I think there's 20. I think there's like 6.

Fraser: But there was a lot of speculation when it first went off that it was actually black students that came into the school and that were shooting everyone else. Right immediately after everyone had run out of the building and were saying, "What the heck are we running from?" people were saying, "I don't know, I just saw some black guy in a trench coat shooting people."

I don't know why people were making the assumption that they were black. But, otherwise at Columbine there is generally not much prejudice or racism.

Hains: I am black/white mixed. And when the media is coming up with this thing that Dylan and Eric were racist, they weren't. They were my friends. They were very nice to me, both of them. I don't get this whole racial thing that people are coming up with.

Adams: Dylan and Eric did use racial slurs. Because, unfortunately, it's becoming common. And what I have heard is they did call Isaiah an N before they shot him. I don't think it meant that they were racist. I think that they were just using the word that they—unfortunately it's true that it has bearing from the movies and TV—that they had learned is okay.

The Nazi Rumors

New York Times: What about the Nazi stuff?

Hains: That is the biggest load of [expletive] I've ever heard. They never wore swastikas around their arm. Never. Not in this entire year that I've known them. No.

Adams: They're not Nazis. They didn't worship Nazis. Some kid said, "Oh I saw them reading a book on Nazis." They read books on Nazis because, guess what they were learning about in World History? They were learning about the Nazis.

Thurman: Everyone said that they saluted to Hitler after a strike in bowling and stuff. That wasn't true. If they got a strike, they would just sit down.

New York Times: The police said Eric's diary was full of Nazi references.

Adams: If Dylan and Eric were like neo-Nazis or whatever, then they kept it secret. They didn't proclaim it. And I don't think Dylan was.

Jackson: I don't think that it was a big racial thing. I mean, you see who they shot at.

New York Times: Is this going to happen in another high school?

Cave: I think that it could happen anywhere. But I think it will happen more. Because, you know, these guys had the courage to do it and so I think there will be followers who will try it, too, or copycats or whatever. And I am like Rich, I am scared to death to go to school.

Fraser: I feel that I'm obligated to go back. I can see for other people who actually had to witness others die, it's understandable that that's probably way too traumatic for them to go back. I can understand that. But I feel like if they were to split up Columbine, or build a new school, then Dylan and Eric would have essentially accomplished their task in breaking up the school.

I think it's going to be tough the first week, or even month, to walk through the halls without remembering what went on. But I think that this school is strong enough and that it's going to be 10 times as good if kids actually stick together.

Jackson: I agree. I want my brother to go back. And I want the students to go back and still compete in whatever they're doing. Because if we don't, then it's going to make me feel like they won. But, it's much greater than that. There's so much love in that school.

New York Times: How well are you dealing with this?

Hains: I was in a drawing class. I saw my friend Lance. He was shot. My teacher would constantly tell him to sit down, sit down, Lance. He was always standing up, walking around talking to everybody.

On Tuesday night I got maybe an hour of sleep, but I had a dream. I was walking into my drawing class and there was Lance. It was just me, Lance and the teacher. And the teacher tells him, "Go sit down, Lance." And he goes over to his desk, sits down, and blows up. And then I see Dylan and Eric laughing. I have never had a worse dream. It's been recurring for the past week. And I just can't get rid of it. Because I've known Lance since middle school. And I've also known Dylan and Eric all year. I'm literally torn between them.

New York Times: Is anyone else having nightmares?

Cave: I haven't had nightmares, but I've hardly been able to sleep in my room. It's in the basement. I've had to sleep on the couch in the living room because I can't go down there at night.

Thurman: I usually just hang out with my friends. We stay up until we pretty much pass out.

New York Times: Did you do that before?

Thurman: No, that's how I do it now. We just hang out until we pretty much cannot stay awake any longer.

New York Times: Is there anything else you want to say?

Fraser: As many times as I've heard it from parents, or counselors, or whoever else, I've never realized as strong as I have now that material possessions really don't mean anything to me anymore. That really the most important thing that you can have in the world is family and friends.

Colbert: I'm just proud to see the community pull together this spiritually. If we could just stay that way, this will never happen again.

Adams: I have one more thing to add. Just three simple words, and we've heard it a lot and it's true. We are Columbine!

Jackson: We will always be Columbine.

Adams: Columbine forever.

To Be an Outsider

Susan Greene

On April 20, 1999, Eric Harris and Dylan Klebold killed twelve students and one teacher at Columbine High School in Littleton,
Colorado, before turning their guns on themselves. After the
killings it was learned that Harris and Klebold were loosely associated with Columbine's clique of outsiders, who were known as the
Trench Coat Mafia. In the following selection, which originally
appeared just days after the shooting, *Denver Post* staff writer Susan
Greene describes a member of the Trench Coat Mafia, who wished
to remain anonymous. The student tells Greene of the daily torment he and other members of the group suffered at the hands of
other students, most notably the athletes. Because they dressed
differently and listened to different music, Greene recounts, members of the Trench Coat Mafia were often singled out for physical
and verbal abuse. According to Greene, the member of the group
whom she spoke to, while not condoning the shootings, says that
he can understand how this unrelenting torment may have
caused Harris and Klebold to snap.

Hell.

The word has been used so often to describe the bloody rampage at
Columbine High School.

But one member of Columbine's now-notorious Trench Coat Mafia
invokes the same image of hell when describing life at the school
before the carnage.

The 18-year-old, who demanded anonymity, said he was taunted
and terrorized by his schoolmates—so-called jocks who called him
"faggot," bashed him into lockers and threw rocks at him from their
cars while he rode his bike home from school.

"I can't describe how hard it was to get up in the morning and face
that," he said.

"Hell," he continued. "Pure hell."

Police repeatedly have questioned the teen about his knowledge of
the shootings.

He is one of several mafia members who at once are shying away

Excerpted from "Teen Describes School Life Filled with Taunts, Abuse," by Susan
Greene, *The Denver Post*, April 24, 1999. Reprinted by permission of *The Denver Post*.

from reporters, but also desperate to have their stories heard.

He and his parents know people will perceive their anonymity as a sign that he has something to hide or in some way is responsible for the massacre.

He's visibly grieving about the tragedy and about what he knows are the ties students are suggesting between him and killers Eric Harris and Dylan Klebold.

The Outcasts

He said the two seniors weren't even part of the mafia, but merely friends of one especially charismatic—and, he notes, the only violent—member.

They were on the fringe of the group, the school's most outcast, most fringe clique.

And so, the teen said, his reluctance to speak out stems not from an association with the shooters, but from the very reason his group of loners banded together in the first place—out of fear of more ridicule and torment, more shoves, more thrown rocks. Or worse.

"I want to stand up and say this is what I went through," he said. "But I'm scared, not just for me, but my family."

By now, most of America and much of the world have heard about Columbine's jocks.

The student-athletes commonly wear clothes bearing the logos of sports teams. Another indication is baseball caps with visors worn facing forward and carefully rounded.

Not all jocks tormented him, the teen noted. But he said a handful of bullies held so much power that most of the school emulated them, or at least were too afraid to voice dissent.

"If you didn't dress like them, if you walked to school or rode your bike, if you didn't get into sports and weren't athletic, then you were an outcast. It's that simple," he said.

The Torment Begins

Taunting started with the teen's appearance which, without compromising his anonymity, is gawky—the painfully uneasy look of so many male teens teetering between boyhood and manhood. He said jocks ridiculed his clothes and his black trench coat, which his parents bought for him to wear with suits on special occasions.

The torment often became vicious.

While the teen biked home from school, he said, jocks would "speed past at 40, 50 mph" and toss pop cans or cups full of sticky soda at him. Sometimes they threw rocks or even sideswiped his bike with their cars.

He described waking on school days with a knot in his stomach and the dread of having to face the humiliation.

He would avoid certain hallways and even make his way to classes outside the school building to escape being ridiculed or being bashed against lockers, he said.

In the cafeteria, he continued, jocks threw mashed potatoes at him. He would wear the stains for the rest of the school day.

But he wasn't the only kid messed with at Columbine. Other mafia members faced similar troubles. And, he said, he knew Klebold and Harris were tormented as well.

The teen speaks about his high school years quietly, but angrily. He's visibly withdrawn and says he's depressed. But he has enough perspective to understand why he joined the mafia. It was the only place he could find friends.

The Trench Coat Mafia

He said the core group of about seven boys—mostly socially awkward kids, loners—started hanging out in 1996. They gradually grew to include more students, boys and girls who called themselves "The Anachronists" because of their interest in the game Dungeons and Dragons and their penchant for Goth, short for Gothic, fashions.

In early 1998, he said, a jock branded them with the name Trench Coat Mafia. The group accepted the moniker, hoping the symbolism would scare their tormenters and that the nefarious aura of a darkly dressed mob would finally give them some peace.

"And it worked," the teen said. "They did start leaving us alone." Members apparently found security in numbers. They hung out together listening to music, watching movies and commiserating about their difficulties at school. Many, he said, were just grateful for the companionship.

Despite widespread news reports about their obsession with the sadist music of Marilyn Manson, he said, only one member really was a fan of the shock-rocker.

The teen also makes a point of noting the group wasn't racist or interested in Nazi history or culture.

"That's so inaccurate, the image that we were like that," he said. "People just want to put labels on us that aren't true."

Harris and Klebold

The teen said Harris and Klebold were less socially active even than other mafia members.

From the outside, he said, they must have seemed part of the group because of their black trench coats and their similar Goth style of dress. But, speaking from the inside, he said they weren't really members. Although they sometimes hung with the mafia in Columbine's commons and shared sneers at the jocks, he recalled, they ate at a separate lunch table and led very separate lives.

Harris and Klebold didn't usually don trench coats, he added, surmising they wore them on the day of the massacre because they helped hide their guns. Further, he noted, theirs weren't really trench coats, but actually Australian dusters—not authentically Goth at all.

The teen is clearly rocked by the massacre. He swallows hard when talking about it, when seeing the yearbook photos of his dead schoolmates and teacher beamed over national TV.

"I'm not saying what they did was OK," he said of Harris and Klebold. "But I know what it's like to be cornered, pushed day after day."

"Tell people that we were harassed and that sometimes it was impossible to take," he told a reporter. "Tell people that . . . eventually, someone was going to snap."

I Understand Why Students Lash Out

William Malverson

In the following selection, William Malverson explains why he identifies with the rage that drove Eric Harris and Dylan Klebold to kill thirteen people at Columbine High School in Littleton, Colorado, in April 1999. Malverson writes that during his high school years he, like Harris and Klebold, was ostracized and abused by classmates to the point where he was only able to react with violence. The massacre at Littleton, Malverson asserts, is the inevitable result of a school system that allows students to freely and viciously abuse one another. Malverson is a computer programmer.

Ever since it happened, the United States has been trying to understand why two good boys in Colorado would want to kill over a dozen classmates, and (apparently) try to destroy their school. Unlike most of the country, I can understand why they would want to do so.

I can understand why they wanted to destroy their school and kill their classmates, because when I was that age, I felt the same way towards my school and classmates. Much like Eric and Dylan, I was an object of constant ridicule from about fifth grade until my high school graduation. I graduated from high school in 1993, but I still carry the scars from public education.

This harassment took innumerable forms. For example, when I was in eighth grade, a pen base that I had worked on in my plastics class, and had just finished polishing, was destroyed by heavy sandpaper when I turned my back for a moment. To this day, I don't know who did it. In twelfth grade, I was told by my locker-mate to find another locker by the end of the day, so that his friend could share "his" locker. If I had the opportunity to do so, even today, I would happily kill him if I knew I could do so without penalty. I've had gum in the hair, "kick me" signs on my back, and just about every other high school harassment that you can think of. I could relate a hundred small stories. No one of them is a tragedy, but taken as a whole, they describe eight years of hell.

Reprinted with permission from "I Understand the Trench Coat Mafia," by William Malverson, available at www.geocities.com/SouthBeach/Lights/4155/TrenchCoatMafia.html.

Lashing Out

More than once, I lashed out. Once, a person bumped into me in the hall, and half a second later found himself thrown against a locker, my hands on his neck in a death grip. I got into a fight and was suspended for three days in eighth grade. The last day of ninth grade, a fellow student smashed an egg on my head. I chased and caught him. Had an administrator not intervened, I would happily have beaten him senseless, and could I have done so, I would have killed him. While I was not particularly physically intimidating, I still remember clearly the adrenaline-enhanced rage I felt at that moment, and believe that I could easily have done it.

When I read about a school shooting, I don't feel the automatic revulsion that most Americans do. Sure, it's tragic when kids die, but I see it as the inevitable result of a school system that allows students to be treated like I was. When a person goes through what I went through, that person is willing to do anything to make it stop. Events like those in Littleton are no different than an abused child or wife finally striking out at the abuser. However, it should be noted that school abuse has the added factor that it is illegal to not go to school. The day after you get beaten up and thrown in a locker, you have to go right back. While some will respond to that with comments about getting back on to horses, it should be pointed out that finally riding a horse has benefits, while there is really nothing to be gained from school abuse.

But these weren't just picked-on kids, you say. They were into Nazism and violent video games. Perhaps. Most kids that age are into violent video games, and any intelligent person is fascinated by the rise and fall of Nazi Germany when he or she first learns of it, which with today's education system could easily not be until high school. I still remember the book on the subject that I read at least a dozen times during the summer of 1989. But they said a racist thing when they shot the black kid, you say. I can understand why they did that as well. I suspect that this was simply one last chance to offend the guy and others around before killing him. This also leaves the white person whose life was spared with a lifetime of knowing that only racist sentiments prevented him from being killed. Both racism and the black boy were psychological tools with which to strike at someone else, nothing more. They've already stepped outside of society's norms by killing a lot of people. Why not step outside those same norms again and use a racist term? Because it's *wrong*? Because they'll have to go to *sensitivity training*?

I suspect that, if anything, high school has gotten worse in the years since I escaped. I shudder to imagine the terror that the unpopular go through today. With the more general breakdown of decency in our society, what few restraints [that] kept me sane are probably gone. Usually, when my teasing had reached a certain point, the others broke it off. I wonder how much farther it has to go today.

A Lesson for the Bullies

Perhaps the teasers and bullies who are now doing to other students what was done to me will realize that you can only go so far with this sort of thing before it backfires. Perhaps "Remember Littleton" will become a rallying phrase for the unpopular students of the world. If just one student has to face less daily ridicule, then these shootings will have had a positive effect.

Do I condone the Colorado killings? No. What these kids did was wrong, and had they been taken alive, I would have fully supported trying them as adults and executing them. Crime must be punished. When a person is pushed so far that they do something like this, it's unlikely that they will ever be able to fit again into normal society, nor should they be given the chance to do so.

I graduated from high school in the spring of 1993. I have moved past my school days, but will never forget them. I remember clearly the day in college, a few months into my first semester, when I realized that, for the first time in close to a decade, I was *content*. Not happy, just content. I was able to go about my business, go to and from class, and go out in public, without having to worry about who I'd have to deal with or avoid, and most of my social interactions were positive. This was something that I had not experienced in a long time.

I don't spend my days obsessing over how popular I was in high school. I have a college degree and a successful computer programming career. Perhaps living well is truly the best revenge. I don't know, and don't want to know, where my old tormentors are. I will never attend a high school reunion.

The Scars

However, I still carry the scars of public education. I am still quite timid. I don't like to express strong opinions or emotions to others, because of a latent fear that I will be teased for them. I still like to blend into a crowd, and don't like to do anything that will draw attention to me. I have trouble making friends, and I never really feel that I can trust the friends I do make to continue to deserve my trust. On some deep-down level, I feel that I must constantly expect them to betray me.

What are the long-term effects of school abuse? I never dated in high school, and only a few times in college. I don't have empathy for other people. I despise the educational system and everything related to it. I agree with something that a friend said to me a while back— "There are a few dozen real people in the world. The rest are scenery." I agree with this statement wholeheartedly. I have a few friends and family members that I care about. I simply ignore, or deal with as little as possible, the rest of the world.

How can we prevent another Littleton? The usual solutions have been trotted out, usually involving getting rid of something that the trotter doesn't like. So far, trench coats, guns, pornography, video games, and music (among others) have been suggested. The real solution is far simpler. Teach our children to treat each other with respect and dignity. Kids like those in the Trench Coat Mafia don't want to be popular. They don't want everyone to like them. They just want to be left alone. If you are a high school student, and want to do something to ensure that this doesn't happen at your school, the solution is very simple. Next time you have the opportunity to tease, harass, or otherwise abuse a student at your school, don't. That's all there is. Don't do it. If you really want to help prevent it, be *nice* to these people who are different than you. Don't patronize them, but just be polite to them. Use as your example the Littleton student who was told, shortly before the shooting began, "We like you. Go home." A little bit of politeness saved that kid's life. A little more, from a few more students, could have saved fifteen more. For example, while I have no idea who destroyed my pen base, I still clearly remember the person who did what he could to fix it in the last twenty minutes of the class. If you're out there, thanks, Dan.

High School Is Hell

"But I don't harass these people!" Perhaps. But teasing is such a faceless thing. Most of the things that were done to me, I have no idea to this day who did them. When you face this sort of thing every day, the world rapidly divides into two groups: The kind of person who teases you, and the kind who does not. Because you can not know who does it, you can only know who does not. The only people you can know do not are your close friends and relatives. Thus, everybody else goes into the "kind of person who teases you" category. Is this fair? Probably not. But neither is the random process that decides which children will be the class outcasts.

To someone who is not accepted by peers, high school is hell. Most people don't truly understand this. Their high school days were filled with friends, fun, and acceptance. To them, high school was truly the best time of their lives. Had I believed that high school was the best time of my life, I probably would have killed myself, and quite possibly in a spectacular manner similar to that of the Littleton shooters.

SIX YEARS OF HORROR

Meredith Minter Dixon

The following selection is taken from Meredith Minter Dixon's Raven Days website, a site that is dedicated to illuminating the problems of bullying and peer rejection in school. Dixon tells the story of her horrific experiences in middle and high school, when she endured almost daily beatings from her fellow students. Though school officials knew of the harassment, the beatings and verbal abuse continued for six years, Dixon writes, and have left lasting scars. The idea that school is a safe place to be is a myth, she explains, but it is such a strong myth that many adults refuse to believe her account of her torment. While Dixon admits that she is at a loss to suggest ways to reduce violent bullying in the schools, she does advocate increased awareness of the problem as a crucial first step.

My elementary school experience wasn't that bad. It was terribly boring, of course—I tested at college level in English when I was nine, and I wasn't far behind that in math—but it was usually physically safe.

On the other hand, when I went to middle school in 1974, it was the start of six years of horror. Status in my middle school was entirely determined by fighting. Status fights were one-on-one and there were rules. But I refused to fight (my mother wouldn't let me hit anyone, for any reason) so the rules didn't apply to me. I wasn't considered human.

In books, the kid who refuses to fight on account of principles is grudgingly respected, if not admired, by the bullies. I can tell you from six years of bitter experience, it doesn't work that way outside of books.

Regular Beatings

In middle school, I was thoroughly beaten up—jumped by a group, knocked to the floor, head pounded on the ground (or the brick, or the concrete), upper body pummeled and sometimes kicked, till I was sick and dizzy and I could barely get back up when they finished—three times a week on average, for two years. I was casually hit or kicked or pushed a few times during most class changes, and people

Excerpted with permission from "Stalag HS," by Meredith Minter Dixon, available at http://web.mountain.net/~dixonm/stalaghs.html.

did small things during class itself—hit or pinched or jabbed with pencils—all the time.

On top of these unscheduled beatings; there were two times a day I could be entirely certain that something would happen. We were required to go to the cafeteria every day for lunch (I know that in some schools kids are allowed to skip lunch; we weren't). In the cafeteria, I couldn't flatten myself against a wall as I would have elsewhere, so I could be hit from all sides. People also often pushed me—"accidentally," of course—into the heating units that kept the food warm in the serving line, and they were hot enough to burn, especially if the person held me against them for a bit. And for a while in seventh grade people made a game of spitting in my food and in my milk. Fortunately they thought of this near the end of the school year, and they'd forgotten about it by the following September.

The worst was gym class. I was jumped every day, regularly as clockwork, at the start of seventh grade gym class. That was worst of all, for several reasons—I had to undress, so I lost the protection of clothing. We had fifteen minutes to dress out, and anyone with reasonable dexterity could dress out in under ten minutes, so they had from five to ten minutes—longer than the average beating—to do whatever they pleased. And the nature of gym class permitted them to inflict worse injuries than they could at other times—it would just be assumed that I got them in class. We all had compasses, not the directional sort, the kind with a sharp point on one end, and my classmates in gym liked to use the points to jab or scratch me (while, naturally, others held me down so I couldn't dodge).

The School Officials Knew

The teachers knew. They were required to stand at their doors and "monitor" the activity in the halls. But I never saw any of them try to break up a fight, much less try to do anything about anyone's hitting the girl who wouldn't hit back. Two of them actually seemed to enjoy seeing other kids hit me; they always watched avidly when someone was doing something to me. The others just looked through me, as though I weren't there.

The administrators knew. I always made a point of going to the office right after my first major beating of the day—not because I thought they'd do anything (I was quite sure they wouldn't) but because the time in the office, while they took the report, would give me five minutes or so to recover from the beating, to stop feeling sick at my stomach and to rearrange my clothes to cushion any abraded place or anywhere that was bleeding—five minutes, before I'd have to go out and be hit again. They never did anything; they never said anything other than "You've got to learn to hit back," or even "You mustn't be scared to hit back."

That last line always astonished and amused me. I was a large, strong girl. I could have fought well enough to be a leader in the school. And if I had fought, I'd never have had to face more than one of the kids at a time, and I'd never have been burned or pushed down the stairs or anything of that kind, because I'd have been considered human and the rules would have applied. And the administrators thought I wasn't fighting because I was "scared"?

The adults knew. The adults did nothing. When a boy broke my arm in eighth grade—he twisted it behind my back and told me to say "uncle"; I didn't say "uncle"—my mother went to school and told them that if I were touched again she'd take me out of school, but unfortunately she never told me this, so I was beaten up many, many times thereafter. The administrators' response was to tell my teachers that they didn't want to hear any reports of my being injured in class (of course, most of the real violence took place during class change or at lunch, where the teachers could always be looking the other way). Several of my teachers responded to this by ordering me to cut class and promising me a guaranteed A if I did so. Others sent me out of the classroom to work alone. One teacher shut me in her coat closet during her class period for the rest of the school year, with the door left open just a crack so I could see the blackboard. Nobody seemed to think of even *asking* the other kids not to hit me; I doubt it would have worked if they had, of course, but it would have been a nice gesture.

The Abuse Continues

In high school, about two-thirds of the kids stopped hitting me and just started ostentatiously shunning me—getting up and moving whenever I sat down at the cafeteria (I could always count on having a table to myself; even if I sat at the very end of a crowded table, and didn't look at them, they'd all get up and leave); scooting their desks away from me, spitting on me; that sort of thing. They'd always propose me for every class office (to the accompaniment of gales of laughter) and the teachers would say, wearily, "'Serious' nominations, please."

I was very lonely, but by high school I was so lonely that I wasn't aware of loneliness, if that makes sense. I had stopped wanting friends because I'd stopped believing that there were such things as friends. It had been so very long since I'd had any, and some of the kids I'd called friends in elementary school had joined the others in middle school in beating me up. . . .

By high school I had it all worked out, philosophically. All societies, I felt, required sacrificial victims to survive, and I was my school's Designated Victim. I never thought of killing them, but I was more than half expecting that they would kill me, sooner or later. They might have done so, too—once my classmates were old enough to drive they liked to drive their cars at me, at some speed, to see me jump into the ditch; if nothing else, one of those times I might have been slow to jump.

If the Littleton killers [on April 20, 1999, Eric Harris and Dylan Klebold shot and killed 12 classmates and one teacher before turning their guns on themselves at Columbine High School in Littleton, Colorado] were indeed neo-Nazis, I don't wonder. I wasn't a neo-Nazi, but World War II did provide me with the best matrix I could find for understanding my situation. Only in the accounts of Nazi Germany did I find any parallels to what my day-to-day life was like. I identified strongly with the heroes of the Resistance—with those who risked torture and with those who suffered it. I read everything I could find about concentration camps and prisoner of war (POW) camps; trying to see how others, adults, had coped with being beaten every day. The stories about the Vietnam POWs were an inspiration to me also, but in 1974 there was more information about World War II.

The Experience Lingers into Adulthood

I thought—how could I not? What other experience did I have?—that this was what adult life would be like, too—that all I had to look forward to was a lifetime of being pushed into walls, of being knocked to the ground and beaten, of going home every day and quietly putting antibiotics on the day's collection of scrapes, scratches, and jabs, or cushioning the worst bruises with cotton. Not knowing that college would be different, I chose my college in part because it had smooth walls, which wouldn't cause abrasions when someone pinned me against them. To this day, twenty years later, I still size up my surroundings, automatically, thinking where the best place to be cornered would be if someone cornered me.

In the wake of the Littleton massacre, I have seen people say and write, over and over again, that the Littleton killers must have been sociopaths, unable to understand that other people had feelings. I've heard people say that the killers must have been unable to reason, that they must have been overreacting to some momentary discomfort.

Not having known either boy (though the others who've commented did not, I presume, know them either) I cannot be sure that these people are wrong. But I think they are wrong. I think that the killers were probably reasoning perfectly well, but reasoning from incomplete data. They probably thought, as I did, that adulthood would be more of the same thing they'd experienced in school. After all, adults always tell children that school is a preparation for life. And, given that misunderstanding, I can understand why they decided to go down fighting.

To any kids who are reading this—I realize it's probably hard for you to believe, but adulthood really isn't like school. It has its own problems, but people don't generally hit you. In the twenty years since I graduated from high school, I've been hit exactly twice. Many adults haven't even been hit that many times. It's a lot safer to be an adult than to be a child. So, if you can, hold on. Senior year will eventually come, and pass, and then, almost unimaginably, you'll be safe.

The School Myth

To any adults—I always swore I'd tell the world what happened to me, as soon as I was an adult and people would listen to me. But as you also know, being an adult doesn't automatically mean that people will listen. People generally haven't listened; they've assumed I must be exaggerating, or lying outright. There's a great myth out there, the idea that school is a good place to be, and it's almost unshakable.

I don't know what we as adults can do to make the schools a good place. I'm not sure it's possible, with graded schools. In chronologically graded schools, there will always be children like me who know all the material in their classes before the first day of class. Even if the schools are made physically safe (and I'm not sure that's possible either) they'll still be a waste of time. In my case, they were worse than a waste; I would have been safer, physically, mentally, and emotionally, spending those years at home, or for that matter working at a job. It's ironic that we've passed so many laws against child labor, for the safety of children, only so that the children can go to a school that is more hazardous than the most hazardous workplace. At least at work people don't usually try to hurt you on purpose.

A Parent's Reaction to a School Bomb Threat

Carolyn Jabs

In the following article, Carolyn Jabs describes her decision to send her son to school despite a bomb threat that occurred shortly after the April 20, 1999, shooting at Columbine High School in Littleton, Colorado, that left fourteen students, including gunmen Eric Harris and Dylan Klebold, and one teacher dead. Her husband was one of many parents who believed the threat was harmless—simply another of the countless threats that schools across America received in the wake of the Littleton shooting. However, Jabs points out that officials and parents at Columbine were criticized for missing clues, much like the bomb threat to her son's school that may have prevented the violent outburst by Harris and Klebold. Though there were no bombs at her son's school that day, writes Jabs, there was no education either because more than half of the students stayed home. Jabs discusses her frustration with how the prankster, despite the absence of a real bomb, was able to disrupt the school day. Jabs is a contributor to *Family PC* magazine.

From the moment I knew I was pregnant with my son, I've taken my studies of parenthood seriously. I read Penelope Leach [a leading child development expert] and T. Berry Brazelton [a premier clinical pediatrician]. I've been to child-rearing seminars as well as P.T.A. meetings. I know about logical consequences and positive discipline. None of it prepared me for the last two weeks.

A Bomb Threat

In mid-May 1999, rumors flew through my son's school that a student had threatened to kill the principal and blow up the sophomores on Thursday, May 27. My son is a sophomore.

Officials at the school took this seriously enough to send a letter to parents, but they decided not to close the school. They hired extra security. All doors but one were to be locked. Book bags were to be searched.

Reprinted from "Littleton's Legacy of Pranks," by Carolyn Jabs, *The New York Times*, June 11, 1999. Copyright ©1999 by The New York Times Co. Reprinted by permission of *The New York Times*.

My husband pointed out that this was simply one of innumerable threats that schools nationwide had received since the shootings in Littleton earlier that month. If schools shut down because of every prank and hoax, he said, we'd all have to start home schooling.

I agreed—until I saw the anxiety on my son's face. When the rumors first started, it seemed like a joke, both to him and to me. He and his friends had wanted to take that Thursday off to visit a local amusement park. But as the date neared, I could tell he no longer thought the whole thing was funny. "I don't think anything will happen," he said as matter-of-factly as he could, "but if it did and I knew ahead of time. . . ."

He was right, of course. Adults in Littleton were criticized for missing "clues." A bomb threat, by contrast, is a neon sign. What would it mean to my son if he believed we put him in danger? How would we live with ourselves if we had?

Held Hostage

On the other hand, if we kept our son home and nothing happened, could we safely send him to school the next day? Life is risky. There have always been disturbed people. And the young people who alert everyone to their intentions probably want to be intercepted.

The day before the threatened attack, I talked to other parents, trying to find a consensus. Instead I discovered a gender gap. Fathers seemed to feel that you can't let your life be held hostage by the actions of an unbalanced person or a malicious prankster. Mothers said, "But it's my child."

By that Wednesday night, we heard rumors that one boy had been arrested and charged with "inciting a panic." It was not clear whether other students were involved. My husband and I still hadn't made a decision about whether to send our son to school.

One by one, my son's friends called to say they wouldn't be going. For a few minutes, we thought about letting our child make this decision for himself, but then we decided it was unfair to turn the problem over to him because we didn't know what to do.

In the end, we sent him to school. We told him we believed the precautions taken by the school would keep him safe. We said he— and we—could not allow deranged people to rule our lives. You have to anticipate risk as best as you can and then go about your business, which in this case, we told him, is education. If courage is doing what you think is right despite inner panic, what we did was courageous.

The Right Decision?

It was a tense day but, in the end, there were no bombs. There was also no education. More than half the students stayed home. Did they act out of genuine fear or because the weather was superb? It's hard to know.

With classes of seven or eight students, teachers showed movies or, in one case, let the kids play Monopoly. My son came home upset not that we'd exposed him to risk but that we'd made him spend pointless time in school when his friends had the day off.

It turned out that an 18-year-old senior and his 15-year-old sister had been arrested earlier that week. It now looks like they were the only students involved, although the authorities didn't know that at the time.

I'm still struggling to find the moral in all this. In retrospect, it seems we were naïve to assume that because the school was open, education would proceed. We acted on principle; the teachers acted on expedience. We still believe that, as parents, we did the right thing. We just wish the teachers had, too.

The Threat Succeeds

As it worked out, what brought education to a halt wasn't teen-age terrorists, but teachers who did not treat the day like any other. Whoever made the threat succeeded in disrupting the entire school, which was probably the intent all along.

Whether or not the teachers taught, we all learned something that day.

Unfortunately, my son learned the futility of being part of a courageous minority. As parents, we learned how easily our best intentions for our child can be sabotaged. For a parent who has taken it all so seriously from the start, it's a lesson learned reluctantly.

A Teacher's Perspective on School Violence

Patrick Welsh

Patrick Welsh, an English teacher at T.C. Williams High School in Alexandria, Virginia, discusses his experiences with school violence and the steps his school has taken to curb violent behavior among students. According to Welsh, school safety depends on the administration's ability to maintain a close working relationship with the local police and to "tune in" to the teen underground network. The administration at T.C. Williams has demonstrated a strong ability to relate with the students, Welsh explains; school officials, through frequent contact and cooperation with the student body, usually learn of a potential conflict and defuse it before it has the chance to escalate. Only through such vigilance and teamwork can school violence be prevented, he writes.

"There's a Code Seven in the cafeteria."

Those are the most unnerving words I ever hear at school. Code Seven means there's a fight going on, and every time the call crackles over the administrators' walkie-talkies, I wonder just how serious it is this time. Another skirmish that's gotten out of hand, or a real disaster? Does anyone have a gun or a knife? After 29 years of teaching English at T.C. Williams [High School in Alexandria, Virginia], Code Seven reminds me of a sore truth: No matter how much I wish it were otherwise, while kids are studying in one area of the school, violence can flare up at any moment in another.

You might think that in a school where there are several fights every month that students would have been worried about their safety the day after the Littleton, Colorado, slaughter in April 1999. When my classes gathered the next morning, I heard shock and anger and reflections about violence. But surprisingly, none of the students told me the killings changed their attitudes about feeling safe in school.

The Students Feel Safe

As one senior, Nonsom Ofulue, told me, "At the ninth-grade center, there were fights every day. I had this weird fascination with them.

Excerpted from "Beyond the Finger Pointing: At My School, We're Trying Harder to Know Our Kids," by Patrick Welsh, *The Washington Post*, April 25, 1999. Reprinted with permission from the author.

Now they make me sick. But . . . I feel school is much safer than being on the street because it's closed off." Another, Andrea Frazao-Castro, asked indignantly, "What right did they have to take all those lives? But I'm not afraid. I think there is less danger in a diverse school where everyone knows someone from another race or culture. . . . It's harder to depersonalize someone as a black or foreigner when they are sitting next to you in class."

What both these girls know is that fights in our school are almost invariably between friends or acquaintances who, as the kids say, "have a beef" with each other. It's white guys fighting other white guys over some perceived slight; it's black girls fighting other black girls over boys. So far, it's never been the thing parents worry about most: some sort of random crazy attack.

But I doubt Ofulue and Frazao-Castro would be so sanguine about their safety were it not for the constant determination of school administrators to keep an eye out for trouble—and their willingness to involve students in confronting the issue. We make no pretense: The possibility of violence is a fact of life here. There is usually a police car—and sometimes two or three—in front of the building. A decade ago, that would have worried parents. Now they appreciate it. The police almost seem like part of the school staff. All of us—administrators, faculty, students and police—are encouraged to see maintaining security as our joint responsibility. . . .

If at night there is a brawl in the community that might spill over into school the next day, the police inform administrators and often show up at school early in the morning. Conversely, administrators let police know about trouble at school that could spill over into the community. But it's not just liaison with the police that administrators value; it's liaison with the kids. Our principal, John Porter, and one of his assistants are out in front of the school nearly every morning greeting students and looking for signs of trouble. From the time students pour off the buses at 7:25 a.m. until they leave at 2:20 p.m., administrators are on the move.

John Porter

Balding and bespectacled, Porter may not appear charismatic, but kids—from nerds to gang members—seem to like and trust him: "If I suspected there was going to be trouble, I'd tell Mr. Porter immediately . . . . He'd take care of things," says Jamar Eubanks, a senior basketball star. The principal is about as plugged into the teen underground network as any adult could be. A few years back, when Porter was greeting kids in the morning, one told him that a boy on another bus had a gun. The cops had that kid—and the gun—within half an hour. In 1998, a possible disaster was averted when a kid told Porter he'd heard a student was making death threats. The cops investigated and found the student had made lists. He was expelled, and put under psychiatric care.

Assistant Principal Robert White is similarly tuned in. When he walked into school in late April 1999, he was hit with a crisis because a fight in the city the night before threatened to escalate in school. That problem consumed his morning as he gathered four kids, their parents, three policemen and another administrator in a conference room to resolve the dispute before it became more serious.

When he got back to his office, students who had been kicked out of classes were lined up to see him; he had several requests from teachers to take care of troublesome kids, parents had left voice messages. And as he worked through it all, he knew that the next day a whole new set of crises would arise. The work is never done.

Student Volunteers

And those two men certainly can't do it alone. Porter has made a point of assembling a team of administrators who get along well—with each other, with teachers and with kids. White helped form a peer-mediation program a few years ago. Now, when two kids have a disagreement, they can go to a special room, and two trained student volunteers are called out of class to mediate. The parties involved give their stories to the volunteers. Neither one is allowed to name call or interrupt the other. When their cases have been stated, the mediators discuss possible resolutions and ask the quarreling students to sign a contract. "It seems that the biggest fights start over the smallest things—the way one looks at someone, third-hand information from the rumor mill, a guy thinking his girlfriend is cheating if she just says hello to another guy. Mediation usually works because [the students] get a chance to hear how the other side feels," says senior Zohra Atmar, one of 35 trained mediators.

While vigilance and teamwork at my school are very good at heading off the one-on-one confrontations or potential gang skirmishes, I don't know if we could have stopped two crazed kids like those in Colorado. But I'd like to think that we would have known about their fascination with death long before it reached the point of no return.

Assistant Principal Robert White is similarly tuned in. When he walked into school in late April 1999, he was hit with a crisis because a fight in the city the night before threatened to escalate in school. That problem consumed his morning as he gathered four kids, their parents, three policemen and another administrator in a conference room to resolve the dispute before it became more serious.

When he got back to his office, students who had been kicked out of classes were lined up to see him; he had several requests from teachers to take care of troublesome kids, parents had left voice messages. And as he worked through it all, he knew that the next day a whole new set of crises would arise. The work is never done.

Student Volunteers

And those two men certainly can't do it alone. Porter has made a point of assembling a team of administrators who get along well—with each other, with teachers and with kids. White helped form a peer-mediation program a few years ago. Now, when two kids have a disagreement, they can go to a special room, and two trained student volunteers are called out of class to mediate. The parties involved give their stories to the volunteers. Neither one is allowed to name call or interrupt the other. When their cases have been stated, the mediators discuss possible resolutions and ask the quarreling students to sign a contract. "It seems that the biggest fights start over the smallest things—the way one looks at someone, third-hand information from the rumor mill, a guy thinking his girlfriend is cheating if she just says hello to another guy. Mediation usually works because [the students] get a chance to hear how the other side feels," says senior Zohra Atmar, one of 35 trained mediators.

While vigilance and teamwork at my school are very good at heading off the one-on-one confrontations or potential gang skirmishes, I don't know if we could have stopped two crazed kids like those in Colorado. But I'd like to think that we would have known about their fascination with death long before it reached the point of no return.

Now they make me sick. But . . . I feel school is much safer than being on the street because it's closed off." Another, Andrea Frazao-Castro, asked indignantly, "What right did they have to take all those lives? But I'm not afraid. I think there is less danger in a diverse school where everyone knows someone from another race or culture. . . . It's harder to depersonalize someone as a black or foreigner when they are sitting next to you in class."

What both these girls know is that fights in our school are almost invariably between friends or acquaintances who, as the kids say, "have a beef" with each other. It's white guys fighting other white guys over some perceived slight; it's black girls fighting other black girls over boys. So far, it's never been the thing parents worry about most: some sort of random crazy attack.

But I doubt Ofulue and Frazao-Castro would be so sanguine about their safety were it not for the constant determination of school administrators to keep an eye out for trouble—and their willingness to involve students in confronting the issue. We make no pretense: The possibility of violence is a fact of life here. There is usually a police car—and sometimes two or three—in front of the building. A decade ago, that would have worried parents. Now they appreciate it. The police almost seem like part of the school staff. All of us—administrators, faculty, students and police—are encouraged to see maintaining security as our joint responsibility. . . .

If at night there is a brawl in the community that might spill over into school the next day, the police inform administrators and often show up at school early in the morning. Conversely, administrators let police know about trouble at school that could spill over into the community. But it's not just liaison with the police that administrators value; it's liaison with the kids. Our principal, John Porter, and one of his assistants are out in front of the school nearly every morning greeting students and looking for signs of trouble. From the time students pour off the buses at 7:25 a.m. until they leave at 2:20 p.m., administrators are on the move.

John Porter

Balding and bespectacled, Porter may not appear charismatic, but kids—from nerds to gang members—seem to like and trust him: "If I suspected there was going to be trouble, I'd tell Mr. Porter immediately . . . . He'd take care of things," says Jamar Eubanks, a senior basketball star. The principal is about as plugged into the teen underground network as any adult could be. A few years back, when Porter was greeting kids in the morning, one told him that a boy on another bus had a gun. The cops had that kid—and the gun—within half an hour. In 1998, a possible disaster was averted when a kid told Porter he'd heard a student was making death threats. The cops investigated and found the student had made lists. He was expelled, and put under psychiatric care.

events, at which disruptive behavior was exceeding the ability of supervisors to maintain a safe and secure environment.

A Different Approach

However, in 1992 the administration decided to take a different tack. Instead of asking the many to pay for the sins of the few, school officials launched a concerted effort to personalize the school experience for that small percentage of students who were engaging in disruptive behavior.

Some of the troublesome students were low achievers, some were members of minority groups, some came from low socioeconomic backgrounds, some had little or no parental support, some were flirting with gangs or had already become full-fledged members. Indeed, they represented a cross section of the school population; no single group was causing the problems, and thus no single group could be the target of the new strategy.

Staff members of Huntington Beach High School picked up the idea of personalization from Theodore Sizer, founder of the Coalition of Essential Schools, who views personalization as the single most important factor that keeps young people in school. When education is personalized, Sizer says, students are known by the adult professionals in the school. Huntington Beach staff members set out to test this theory.

The vice principal of supervision, the school psychologist, the school nurse, and the community outreach liaison all compiled "hot lists" of students whom they viewed as not on track to graduate because of behavior problems. Meanwhile, all Huntington Beach faculty members were asked to jot down the names of their "top 10" students—the ones who seemed to need extra attention—and the district office was asked to furnish a list of all Huntington Beach High School students who had received three or more F's on their latest report card. The names on the various lists were cross-referenced, and staff members started getting to know these youngsters by name.

The Adopt-a-Kid Program

First, an adopt-a-kid program was initiated, which matched adult volunteers on campus with one or two students of their choosing from the list. The adults were to listen, to provide information when needed, and to provide support or advice when asked. The adults met with the students before school, after school, over lunch, or—when appropriate—during class. To ensure frequent contact, several of the teachers appointed these students as their class aides. Others met with their students only a few times but nonetheless functioned as campus adults who knew the students by name and greeted them every time they saw them. Attempts were made to match students' learning styles with the adults' personality styles. This simple-to-implement program cost the school and its cash-strapped district nothing, since it relied on the efforts of volunteers.

At the same time, the vice principal, the assistant principal, the school psychologist, the school nurse, the community outreach liaison, and selected staff members formed a group that met weekly to discuss the progress of students on the list. This group functioned much like a student study team, but its efforts were not limited to special education students. The weekly meetings enabled all staff members who dealt with student services to talk to one another and compare notes, thus ensuring that the left hand knew what the right hand was doing.

The principal instituted "most improved student" awards, which were given each quarter. Every teacher submitted the names of the boy and the girl who had shown the most improvement in that teacher's classes during the quarter. These students were then called out of class to receive their awards in person from the principal. They were given key chains with their names on them (provided by the Parent/Teacher/Student Association), certificates, and letters for their parents. The principal read the personal comments the teachers had written about these students. Many youngsters on the adopt-a-kid list received "most improved student" awards.

The administration maintained a "student of the month" program, which honored outstanding students by placing their names on the school marquee and in the principal's newsletter to parents. An "athlete of the month" program was begun as well.

A student forum was held twice each month in the principal's conference room, open to any student who wished to discuss a school activity or policy or to voice a complaint. The vice principal chaired the forum, demonstrating that students' ideas have value and ensuring that school officials would give them serious consideration.

A Zero-Tolerance Campaign Against Violence

The principal started a "green-ribbon campaign" to promote awareness of and to express a zero-tolerance attitude toward violence on campus. Every Tuesday throughout the school year, staff members and students wore little green ribbons (provided by the Parent/Teacher/Student Association) to show their antiviolence stance. The program was voluntary; students had to come to the office to request green ribbons. Yet, within a month, students were sporting green ribbons everywhere, from their hair to their shoelaces.

Over a period of about two months, the principal collected headlines from local newspapers that suggested an increase in violent acts within the community. He then assembled a panel composed of a juvenile court judge, a probation officer, a local detective, local police officers, and a Los Angeles mother whose son had been killed by gangland gunfire. Instead of packing all 2,050 students into the gym for the panel's presentation, he had students assemble with their English classes in the more intimate auditorium—roughly 250 students per period. In this setting, the students learned how the justice and penal systems deal with illegal and violent acts, and they were touched by the mother's personal account of the pain of senseless violence.

During the first year of the personalization effort at Huntington Beach High School, the student government spent a significant sum to provide each student with a folder—printed in school colors—containing school rules, regulations, and policies. The folders were distributed during physical education classes. But the vice principal noticed that trash cans outside the gymnasium were literally overflowing with these handsome folders at the end of the day on which they were issued.

Thus, during the first two weeks of the second year, administrators went to every English class to hand a folder to each student and to spend the period discussing the contents. Students were encouraged to ask questions about the source of each rule—whether from the education code, from district policy, or from school policy. For all intents and purposes, the administrative offices were shut down during this interval of visiting English classes, but not a single folder has been sighted in a trash can since.

The Personal Approach Yields Results

Who's to say which of these initiatives was most influential in curbing violence and suspendable offenses at Huntington Beach High School? One thing is certain: the 1992–93 school year was different. The school had the lowest expulsion rate (only one student) and the lowest suspension rate in the entire district. Fifty-one percent of the students on "the list" improved their grade-point averages. At the same time, on the district's annual senior survey, seniors at Huntington Beach High gave their school the highest overall grade-point average of any senior class in the district. (There are six comprehensive high schools and one continuation school in the district.) This was a first for Huntington. Test scores also rose, probably a reflection of the greatly improved climate on campus. At the 1993 spring dance, which was held on a ship, the ship's personnel commented that Huntington students had been the best-behaved of all student groups using the ship that year.

During the 1993–94 school year, Huntington Beach saw a 47% decrease in suspensions over the previous year and "the list" was 51% shorter—even from the very first grading period. The adopt-a-kid program was expanded to include peer assistant leaders (PALS), to be sure that students at risk knew other students as well as adults. The improved climate on campus gave staff members the confidence to try block scheduling (which they later voted overwhelmingly to continue during the 1994–95 school year) and other progressive restructuring ideas. Under block scheduling, teachers see only 90 students a day (for longer periods of time), rather than dealing with 180 students a day in 50-minute periods. This allows teachers to work more closely with individual students, despite the large average class size of 39 at Huntington High. Student behavior at all school events, including graduation, was the pride of the district. And—to top off the 1993–94 school year—Huntington Beach High was named a 1994 California Distinguished School.

No frills. No new funds. No grants. Just some simple, low-cost efforts to personalize have yielded dramatic improvements at Huntington Beach High.

BULLYING CAN BE PREVENTED

Frank J. Barone

Contrary to popular belief, writes Frank J. Barone, bullying is not a rite of passage; if left unchecked, it can lead to tragic consequences. However, he asserts, bullying can be prevented by improving teacher supervision of the areas where it is most likely to occur, as well as by training teachers to recognize bullying when it happens. In addition to increased teacher awareness of bullying, Barone explains, bullies must be held accountable for their behavior. If students see that bullying is dealt with sternly, more victims will come forward to report it, Barone points out. Barone is the principal of Amsterdam High School in New York.

Almost everybody can tell a story or two about having once been victimized in school by a bully. Many people can discuss in detail the incidents surrounding the experience and can even remember the name of the bully and the grade level at which the trauma occurred. Few of us go through all the years of schooling unscathed. And while most of us get over the fear and the humiliation, some do not.

Nathan Feris, a seventh-grader at DeKalb High School in DeKalb, Missouri, decided that enduring four years of taunting by other children, who called him "chubby" and "walking dictionary," was more than enough. On 2 March 1987 Feris brought a gun to school and fatally shot another student before turning the gun on himself in class. Classmates said that nobody really had anything against Nathan. "He was just someone to pick on," they said.

A set of parents in Japan have filed a 22-million-yen damage suit against the Tokyo metropolitan government and the parents of two alleged bullies, claiming that their 13-year-old son's suicide was caused by ijimi (bullying). The parents also claim that the school principal and several teachers not only failed to intervene to stop the harassment, but actually assisted the bullies in their activities. The boy hanged himself in a railway rest room and left a note naming two classmates as the cause of his anguish.

It seems that bullying has been a problem in schools for as long as there have been schools. Why is this so? Although not encouraged, bullying continues to be a problem for many children because it is

Excerpted from "Bullying in School: It Doesn't Have to Happen," by Frank J. Barone, *Phi Delta Kappan*, September 1997. Reprinted with permission from the author.

widely tolerated. Teachers, school officials, parents, and other students too often seem to stand by as children are degraded, humiliated, beaten, and ridiculed.

Left unchecked, bullying in school can lead to tragic consequences akin to the two cases mentioned above. Even when suicide or murder is not the outcome, bullying can leave lasting emotional and psychological scars on children. Furthermore, research has shown that bullying can extend across the generations: the children of bullies often become bullies themselves.

Why, then, do school officials, teachers, and parents often appear to take so little notice? One reason may be because many adults consider bullying to be a normal part of growing up. Confronting a bully is considered one of the "rites of passage" for a boy. Unfortunately for the victim, the age-old advice to "stand up to" the bully and fight back usually leads to more violent bullying. Rarely does the bully back down. A second reason why bullying continues unabated might be that educators have become desensitized to bullying and do not even see it. Thus they seldom report it. A third reason could be that the schools are overwhelmed by other issues and problems outside of education with which they must deal. And finally, schools may not want to identify bullying as a problem because they do not have the resources to address it.

Scope of the Problem

Students who are the victims of bullies and school officials who hold the power to stop them have very different perceptions of the problem. This difference has hindered effective prevention efforts.

I developed a survey that was administered in spring and summer of 1993 to two groups in upstate New York. The first group consisted of 847 eighth-graders; the second group consisted of 110 counselors, teachers, and administrators in the same schools as the students. The survey contained the following definition of bullying: "Bullying is a situation when a student or group of students is mean to you over a long period of time (weeks or even months). Bullying can either be physical (hitting, kicking, and so on) or it can be verbal (threats, name calling, gossiping, or ignoring)." Using this definition, the school staff members were asked to estimate the percentage of the "students in their schools" who had been victimized by bullying. On average, the staff members believed that 16% of the students had been victims of bullies. The students in the same schools were asked whether they had "ever been bothered by a bully or bullies while you were in middle school." And 58.8% of the students surveyed said that they had.

The size of the difference in perceptions between students and school staff members suggests that the staff members do not recognize the extent of the bullying that students face. Bullying just does not seem to be "that big a problem" to the staff.

The same survey uncovered some interesting facts. Contrary to what many of us believe, bullying in school does not primarily involve boys. Popular portrayals, such as *The Lord of the Flies* and *The Lords of Discipline*, which depict only boys as both the bullies and the victims, do not reflect reality. As shown in this study, only 47% of the victims of bullying in middle school are boys. Thus, according to the students' own perceptions, the majority (53%) of the victims of bullies are girls.

Not surprisingly, the bullying that takes place among boys tends to be more physical (punching, kicking, pushing, and so on) than that which takes place among girls (which is usually more verbal in nature). Among the students who said that the bullying they had experienced was mostly physical, 89.3% were boys. Among those students who said that the bullying they experienced was mostly verbal, 67.1% were girls.

Among all students surveyed, 10% indicated that they had been physically injured by a bully in school. Furthermore, the nature of the injuries ranged from minor bumps and bruises to some injuries that required hospitalization. Of those students who said they had been injured by a bully, 76.5% were boys.

Effective Remedies

When asked to name the three most effective ways of solving the bullying problem in school, most staff members named "tougher discipline" (41.4%), followed by "better supervision" (33.7%). Only 17.4% of staff members listed "more counseling." Students, on the other hand, mentioned "more counseling" most often (43.2%); 25.8% mentioned "tougher discipline," while 22% mentioned "better supervision."

Tougher discipline is clearly important. Bullies must be held accountable for their behavior, or the behavior will continue. Victims will come forward if they can see that bullies are dealt with sternly, and bullies will be deterred.

Schools also need to improve their supervision efforts. This does not necessarily mean having more supervision, but rather making certain that the correct areas are supervised. Most adult survey respondents said that they believed bullying tends to occur in out-of-the-way and hard-to-supervise places, such as on playgrounds and in locker rooms. But 62.9% of the students surveyed indicated that most bullying in their school occurs in the hallways. (Only 10.6% of the staff surveyed felt that most of the bullying in their school takes place in the hallways.) Staff members need to improve the ways they supervise school hallways. Teachers can do this effectively by situating themselves in the doorways of their classrooms during passing time. Teachers also need to be taught what to look for when monitoring for bullying. What teachers may interpret as accidental pushing and shoving in a crowded hallway may in fact be deliberate and premeditated bullying.

Finally, schools need to invest in inservice training for staff members and in counseling programs that counsel victims and bullies alike. Several programs exist that do so. Some involve large-group sensitivity training, while others interweave the issue of bullying into the curriculum.

Intervention Programs

The most widely known intervention for bullying has been used in Norway by Daniel Olweus. The main goal of the program is to reduce the incidence of bullying in schools. It educates teachers, other school officials, and parents about bullying through a 32-page booklet that was distributed to all schools in Norway. Olweus describes the keys to the program's success: 1) creating a school environment characterized by warmth, positive interest, and involvement with adults; 2) setting firm limits on unacceptable behavior; 3) consistently applying sanctions against bullying; and 4) having adults act as authority figures.

In Olweus' program adults closely supervise recess and enforce "strict and straightforward" rules of behavior. School officials mete out consistent, nonphysical punishment to children who misbehave in aggressive ways. Rewards and praise are also part of the program. Parents are encouraged to teach their children to develop and maintain friendships. Though Olweus believes that the peer group can play an important role in discouraging bullying, he places the main responsibility for dealing with bullies on the adults in the school.

Erling Roland, also of Norway, has offered his own suggestions for dealing with bullies. The first involves having a class read and discuss a story about bullying. The second asks students to hand in written work that deals with a child's feelings and thoughts about being bullied. The third approach involves role-playing, often reversing the role of the bully and the victim. A fourth approach involves the use of peer sponsors, who are students who assume responsibility for looking after younger children. And finally, Roland discusses the use of class meetings in which the group assumes responsibility for the well-being of all its members.

An evaluation of Olweus' model was conducted in Bergen, Norway. After 20 months of implementation, the number of students who reported being bullied declined by 50%, and there was a general reduction in other antisocial behaviors, such as vandalism, theft, and truancy.

Caroline St. John-Brooks describes a school in North London where the head teacher has made a point of attempting to reduce bullying by encouraging all students to tell someone when they have been bullied. Students new to the school are told: "You have a right to come to school without being afraid. This is a 'telling school.' The rule that you must not tell was invented by bullies, and you will only get into trouble if you don't tell."

D. Stead reports that some British schools have established "bully courts" to deal with bullying behaviors. Once a week the court, made up of a faculty advisor and four students, convenes to read descriptions of bullying behavior and mete out such punishments as after-school detention and eating lunch in isolation.

Andrew Mellor's 1990 study, *Bullying in Scottish Secondary Schools,* outlines some proven strategies for combating bullies. First, the school must acknowledge that the problem exists and that it hurts students. Second, victims will not come forward unless bullying is unequivocally condemned throughout the school. Finally, parents, teachers, and pupils need to be involved in formulating an anti-bullying policy so that they will have a vested interest in making it succeed.

Stuart Greenbaum [cofounder of the National School Safety Center] lists and discusses 10 prevention and intervention strategies that schools can employ to deal with bullying:

1. Use a questionnaire to determine the scope of the problem.
2. Communicate clear standards of behavior, and consistently enforce them.
3. Monitor playgrounds closely.
4. Establish a recording system for incidents of bullying.
5. Provide children with opportunities to discuss bullying.
6. Never overlook intentionally abusive acts.
7. Contact the parents of both the victims and the bullies when a problem occurs.
8. Establish intervention programs.
9. Encourage parent participation.
10. Provide support and protection for victims.

It is important to recognize that bullying does not have to be part of a child's school experience. It is not "part of growing up," nor is it a "rite of passage." By working together, schools and parents can make going to school an experience that students will enjoy, not dread.

THE RETURN OF SCHOOL UNIFORMS

Jessica Portner

In the following selection, Jessica Portner describes the mandatory-uniform policy adopted by the Long Beach, California,
school district in 1994. Since the policy went into effect, Portner
notes, the number of assaults, fights, and suspensions in the
school district has dropped dramatically. Uniforms reduce unde-
sirable behavior because they put students in the right frame of
mind to learn, writes Portner. Uniforms also make intruders easier to identify and reduce student violence associated with the
wearing of gang colors, she points out. Though some students
and parents have complained of the added expense and the
monotony of the uniform policy, Portner explains that most
have embraced school uniforms as a positive measure to increase
school safety. She also reports that other school districts across
the United States are implementing or considering similar policies. Portner is an assistant editor for *Teacher Magazine*.

Linda Moore has been feeling especially proud lately.

And she has President Clinton to thank.

In his State of the Union Address in 1996, Mr. Clinton praised student uniforms as a way to promote safety and discipline in public
schools. Ms. Moore, the principal of Will Rogers Middle School, felt a
particular satisfaction in the endorsement.

"Everybody is looking for answers, and here is a district that is
doing something that is working," she said. Since 1994, the 83,000-
student Long Beach system has required its elementary and middle
school students to dress in uniform fashion. It was the first public
school district in the nation to do so.

Mr. Clinton may have had this Southern California school system
in mind when, in his speech, he challenged public schools to mandate uniforms "if it meant that teenagers [would] stop killing each
other over designer jackets."

Since the mandatory-uniform policy was launched in 56 elementary and 14 middle schools here in fall 1994, violence and discipline
problems have decreased dramatically, a survey by the district shows.

Excerpted from "Uniforms Get Credit for Decrease in Discipline Problem," by Jessica
Portner, *Teacher Magazine*, vol. 15, no. 21, February 14, 1996. Reprinted with permission from *Teacher Magazine*.

From the year before uniforms were required, 1993–94, to 1995, assault and battery cases in grades K–8 have dropped 34 percent. Physical fights between students have dropped by 51 percent, and there were 32 percent fewer suspensions.

Though each school in the district can choose its own uniform, most Long Beach students are required to wear black or blue pants, skirts, or shorts with white shirts. Nearly 60,000 K–8 students are affected by the policy.

Parents have the option of excusing their children from the requirement. But, so far, only 500 parents have filled out petitions to exempt their children, according to Dick Van DerLaan, a spokesman for the district.

In addition to Long Beach, a few other districts in California and across the country are testing the benefits of requiring students to come to school in color-specific, and sometimes style-specific, clothing.

The Oakland, California, schools began a similar uniform policy in September 1995. And a small number of other districts—including Dade County, Florida; Seattle; and Charleston, South Carolina—allow schools to decide for themselves whether to require uniforms.

But Long Beach appears to be the first school system to have documented measurable success in improving student behavior.

Since students at Rogers Middle School started wearing black bottoms, white tops, and red jackets or sweaters, fights have declined by 40 percent, and academic performance has improved, school officials said.

Uniforms are an effective method of reducing unwanted behavior, she said, because the more formal clothing puts students in the right mind-set to learn.

Dressing for Success

"It's about dressing for success," said Ms. Moore, who said she wears the school uniform as a gesture of solidarity with her students. She has a selection of bright red blazers in her home closet.

Not one parent at Rogers Middle School has opted out of the plan in 1996, and a quick look around campus at the unbroken stream of red, white, and black shows that students are largely compliant. But there are some exceptions.

In February 1996, as Ms. Moore darted down the hall between classes, the former basketball coach was scanning the crowds.

"Tuck in that shirt," she called out to one disheveled teenager who was slouching against a locker. She looked disparagingly at another whose sweatshirt was clearly purple, not red.

In addition to choosing uniform colors, each of the district's schools is allowed to chose the fabric and style of dress. One elementary school requires its pupils to wear ties, and a few others prefer plaid, but most stick with blue or black and white.

"This isn't a private, prep school, with a coat-of-arms and saddle shoes look," Mr. Van DerLaan said. "It's a little more California casual."

Generation Gap

A catalyst for adopting uniforms in Long Beach was parents' fears over students being attacked for inadvertently wearing a wrong color scarf or hat that might provoke rivalry among local gangs.

The district adopted a dress code more than a decade ago that prohibits gang-related attire, as well as caps, bandanas, baggy pants, and electronic pagers. But many felt the district had to take a more drastic approach.

When Judy Jacobs had two children attending Rogers Middle School, she was among the organizers of the effort to bring uniforms to that school. She now has a child in a district elementary school and has remained enthusiastic about uniforms. "There are so few boundaries for kids these days, with the drug use and violence, so if we can give them some limits, that's good," she said.

The uniformity tends to bolster safety because it makes it easier to spot people who may not belong on campus, school leaders say.

Many who teach in areas where gangs are prevalent argue that students are safer walking to school when dressed in uniform.

"If gang members see one of our students in uniform, they'll leave them alone," as if they belong to a different clique, said Wilma Ferguson, who has been a gym teacher at Franklin Middle School here for 14 years.

But a large portion of the district's students aren't as upbeat as parents and teachers appear to be. And the older they get, the less they seem to like it—which may not bode well for talk in the district of expanding the uniform requirement to high schools.

"It's like we're all in jail," said Hector Gonzalez, a 7th grader at Rogers.

"It's totally bogus," said Gan Luong, an 8th grader at Franklin. "If you wear decent clothes, you shouldn't have to wear uniforms."

Alicia Nunez, also an 8th grader at Franklin, complained that the regimented attire stifles her creativity. "You come to school to get your education, not for them to tell you how to dress," the 14-year-old said as she strode across campus wearing a chocolate-brown T-shirt and jeans.

Legal Challenge

The U.S. Supreme Court hasn't directly addressed the question of whether public schools can impose dress requirements on their students. Lower courts, however, have generally upheld school dress codes.

In the fall of 1995, in one of the first legal tests of a mandatory-uniform policy, an Arizona state judge upheld a Phoenix middle school's policy, even though it does not give students the right to opt out of the requirement.

Most public schools and districts offer a parent or guardian the opportunity to excuse a child from wearing a uniform. And most do not impose harsh penalties on students who are supposed to wear uniforms but don't.

"Schools generally feel they need to exercise latitude when they put their foot down," said Gary Marx, a spokesman for the American Association of School Administrators in Arlington, Virginia.

The American Civil Liberties Union of Southern California, on behalf of a group of low-income families, filed a lawsuit in state court in October 1995 against the Long Beach Unified School District, claiming that the district's uniform policy is a financial burden on poor families. The ACLU also claimed that the district has violated state law by neglecting to adequately inform parents about their right to exempt their children from the program.

The law signed in 1994 by California Governor Pete Wilson to allow state public schools to require uniforms also says that parents must have a way to opt out of such requirements.

The ACLU lawyers say many parents can't afford the cost of school uniforms. About 66 percent of the district's elementary and middle school students qualify for free or reduced-price lunches. [In a February 1996 settlement, the plaintiffs agreed that the district had the right to require school uniforms, provided there is adequate notice, uniform assistance for disadvantaged pupils, and an exemption procedure.]

Hope Carradine, who dresses three of her five children in uniforms, said she had to ask other family members to help pay for them. "I shop thrift and buy in bulk, and you can't do that with uniforms," she said.

Other Strategies

But district officials say that parents can buy the essential items—a white shirt and a pair of pants—for $25 from several area stores. In addition, many schools sell sweatshirts or shorts for $6 each. Many local charities also provide free uniforms, backpacks, and shoes to needy students.

And if parents find the costs too burdensome, Mr. Van DerLaan, the district spokesman, said, they can always opt out. A flier explaining this right was sent to parents nine months before any uniform policies became effective, he said.

Despite their commitment to the school-uniform policy, Long Beach officials don't view it as a panacea for discipline problems.

Other efforts, such as stepped-up parent involvement and additional conflict-resolution classes also have contributed to the more peaceful climate on campuses, school leaders here say.

The district is continuing to evaluate the benefits of uniforms to determine whether 1995's improved numbers for behavior were more than a blip on the screen.

And while some Long Beach students complain that the regulation dress is monotonous and dampens their personal style, many also see a positive side.

"The good thing is people judge you on your inner characteristics rather than what you wear," said Nick Duran, an 8th grader and the student-body president at Rogers Middle School. Plus, he said, it's easier to choose what to put on in the morning.

PROTECT THE CHILDREN

Stephen Winn

In the following article, Stephen Winn, deputy editorial page editor of the *Kansas City Star,* describes the necessity of increasing
the level of security in schools, especially since the April 1999
incident in which Eric Harris and Dylan Klebold killed themselves
and thirteen others at Columbine High School in Littleton, Colorado. In an attempt to prevent similar violent episodes, according to Winn, a number of schools are hiring armed guards,
installing metal detectors, and issuing identity cards that are to be
worn at all times. Although measures such as gun control, greater
awareness of media violence, and counseling for the mentally
unbalanced should be pursued as well, they will require years to
yield results, Winn explains, while tighter security measures on
school grounds can be effective immediately.

When a crazed white supremacist went looking for victims in Los
Angeles [on August 10, 1999, Buford O. Furrow shot five people at a
Jewish community center], he repeatedly ran into a serious obstacle:
Tight security measures.

The would-be mass murderer reportedly checked out a museum, a
cultural center and the University of Judaism. But he decided against
attacking each of them because of their security systems.

Tough Measures Make a Difference

There is a crucial lesson here for school boards, superintendents and
college administrators in the Kansas City area and around the country
as they prepare for the coming school year:

Tough, no-nonsense security measures can make a difference. Not
always. But sometimes.

And while the killer may go elsewhere to wreak havoc, as was the
case in Los Angeles, good security systems can delay the attacks and
perhaps alert authorities in time to prevent tragedy.

A *New York Times* report on August 13, 1999, summarized the steps
that many school districts and universities across the country are tak-

ing in response to recent mass killings, particularly the slaughter in April 1999 at a Colorado high school.

Many schools are hiring armed guards, installing metal detectors, removing lockers, issuing identity cards, controlling entrances and taking other measures that would make it harder for someone to enter buildings with weapons.

American society cannot rely entirely on such measures. We need better gun control, less media violence and greater awareness of the threats posed by extremist groups.

Perhaps most important—the evidence on this point is overwhelming—we need to ensure that people receive appropriate help when they are suffering from mental illnesses that can lead to violence against themselves or others.

An Immediate Solution

But these are broad, long-range solutions that will require years and years of sustained effort. In the more immediate future, millions of parents will soon be sending their children off to school again.

We understand that there are far more hazardous places in American society than the schools. But the schools are where our children spend much of their time.

Many of those children, after the horrendous news stories in recent months, are themselves anxious about their safety.

So as the schools open in the coming weeks, we parents hope to see solid security systems in place.

If we don't see them, we should be asking why.

Unfortunately, advocates of greater security in the schools run into two basic attitude problems:

School systems, like other institutions, often suffer from knee-jerk resistance to change.

Parents around the country have been saying for years that more secure school environments rank at the top of their priority lists.

But many educators have simply shrugged this off.

The Excuses

If you talk to professional educators and school board members about security, you soon run into an array of misinformation and lame excuses:

We don't have enough money. We are too busy. Our school buildings have too many doors to secure. Metal detectors won't do any good. We don't want to be too rigid. You can't stop someone bent on destruction. We live in—take your pick—a safe city, a safe suburb, a safe rural area, a safe middle-class area, a safe upper-class area.

The "too expensive" argument is particularly annoying. Too expensive compared to what?

Are we to believe that everything a school system is currently doing is more important than better security? That no priorities need to be rearranged, no staff positions reassessed?

Even high-quality security systems are not foolproof. But many educators are too quick to dismiss their effectiveness.

"Parents will call up and ask if a school has metal detectors," complains Dennis Lewis, a school administrator in Springfield and vice president of the National Association of School Safety and Law Enforcement Officers, in the *Times*. "All of us know that no metal detector is going to stop someone who wants to shoot in a school."

No, all of us do not know that.

Perhaps some of the parents who called about metal detectors remembered that a security system built around metal detectors proved to be a critical obstacle for a deranged gunman in the nation's capitol [on July 24, 1998, Russell Eugene Weston shot and killed two people and wounded one other in Washington, D.C.].

Out of Place?

The other attitude problem involves ordinary people who just don't like the idea of metal detectors, guards and other stringent security measures in the schools.

Such things, they say, just seem out of place in the schools.

But the violence in our society cannot simply be wished away.

Prudent security measures are not the problem. They are part of the solution.

Many companies and government offices are protected by elaborate security systems. So are airline flights. So are shopping centers and parking lots.

Many adults demand strong security for themselves as they go about their business every day.

Yet we have been slow—remarkably slow—to provide similar protection for young people.

THE CLASSROOM IS BECOMING A POLICE STATE

Michael Easterbrook

In the following selection, Michael Easterbrook, a contributor to *Psychology Today,* questions the effectiveness of some of the heightened security measures that have been adopted by many schools in the wake of several school massacres. While Easterbrook agrees that schools should take precautions to prevent such massacres, he warns that spiked fences, metal detectors, and blast-proof doors and windows—along with a heightened sense of suspicion—are making American schools look and feel more like prisons. Neurological and psychological research has determined that placing students in a prisonlike atmosphere adversely affects their cognitive abilities, Easterbrook explains. Moreover, he writes, placing troubled students in an atmosphere that resembles a police state may actually fuel their fascination with guns, increase their resistance to authority, and spur their violent tendencies.

Tension in the classroom had been building all year. The English teacher was fresh out of college, and her pupils, about 15 of them, were seniors on the advanced-placement track at South Fayette High School outside of Pittsburgh, Pennsylvania. These stellar students weren't accustomed to pulling grades below an A, but the teacher was infuriatingly tough, frequently returning papers marked C and D. "It was kind of like a little war," says Matt Welch, the class president and one of the students. "It just seemed like she was out to get us."

If there was one person the teacher really seemed to have it in for, it was Aaron Leese. A bold 18-year-old with short red hair, Leese was popular with his classmates, if not exactly your model student. Police had busted him in the park with a bottle of bourbon. In school, he had a habit of embarrassing the teacher by asking her questions in front of the class that she found hard to answer. Leese also didn't take kindly to low marks on his assignments. Once, he was so riled by a grade that the teacher asked him to leave. As he was walking out he muttered something like "troglodyte bitch," which earned him a three-day suspension.

Mad Enough to Kill?

The relationship between the two became increasingly strained. One morning in spring, she handed back one of the year's last big assignments, a 10-page essay on a book of one's choice. Leese had written his on Thomas Moore's *Utopia*. He needed an A to pass the class, but he received a D. "I said, 'Man, if I don't pass this class, I'm going to be mad enough to kill,'" Leese recalls. "It was something I said out of frustration. After that the teacher said, 'That could be misinterpreted, you know?' I said, 'Yeah, my bad. I take it back.'"

The exchange went so quickly that a student who sat directly behind Leese didn't even catch it. But it made a distinct impression on the teacher. After class ended, she reported it to the principal, who pulled Leese into his office and phoned the police. By noon, Leese was being escorted off school grounds by two officers from the South Fayette Township Police Department. He was now facing criminal charges. "I was in tears," Leese says.

Had Leese made his comment just five years ago instead of in spring 1998, it might well have gone unnoticed. But a string of deadly shootings at schools around the country is radically altering how these institutions interact with their students. Since February 1996, the massacres, seven in all, have left a total of 35 students, teachers and principals dead. In the latest tragedy at Columbine High School in Littleton, Colorado, two youths killed 13 before taking their own lives.

Alarmed by such incidents, educators are changing the way they go about their mission—and the steps some are taking go far beyond a heightened sensitivity to violent language. They're installing spiked fences, metal detectors, emergency alert systems. They're hiring security guards and imposing searches of students' bags, lockers and desks. And they're insisting that teachers learn skills not included in any syllabus: how to run lock-down drills, how to strip a student vigilante of his weapon.

Disturbing Questions

No one would deny that educators have a right—make that an obligation—to do all they can to protect themselves and their charges from what has become a prime threat to their safety: students themselves. But worrisome questions have arisen about the effects such measures are having on the education which is the schools' purpose to provide. More disturbing still are suggestions that the efforts may not be effectively preventing trouble—and may even be promoting it.

The change most immediately apparent to students has been the move to punish those who use violent language. It's hard to fault administrators for paying close attention to such outbursts. Reporters delving into the lives of the young killers invariably have surfaced with tales of suspicious remarks made before the carnage. Like Barry Loukaitis, the 14-year-old who killed two students and a teacher at

Frontier Middle School in Moses Lake, Washington, who told a friend how cool it would be to go on a shooting spree. Or Kip Kinkel, accused of killing four people at Thurston High School in Springfield, Oregon, who talked frequently of shooting cats, blowing up cows and building bombs. And more recently still, Eric Harris, one of the Columbine shooters, who posted a message on the Internet saying, "You all better hide in your houses because I'm coming for everyone, and I will shoot to kill and I will kill everyone."

Remarks like these, recalled with remorse after the fact, have led principals and teachers to be on the lookout for more of the same. But when do such comments represent an actual intent to kill, and when are they merely the product of an active fantasy life?

Going Too Far

Robby Stango, for example, was a 15-year-old freshman at Kingston High School in upstate New York in May 1998 when school officials were alerted to a poem he had written for a class assignment. Titled "Step to Oblivion," the poem is about a divorced man who decides one night to jump off a cliff and end his life. "Here I am/Standing here on this gloomy night/Minutes away from my horrid fate," the verse begins. The precipice is only seven feet high, however, and the man survives the fall. "Maybe my prayer was answered/Or it could have been just luck/But I was given a second chance at life," the poem concludes.

Despite its positive ending, the verse convinced school officials that Stango was headed for trouble. Although the teen was seeing a counselor at the time about problems he was having at home, he didn't pose a danger to himself or others, according to therapists familiar with his case. Yet the school's discovery of the poem set off a chain of events that resulted in Stango being forced, against his mother's wishes, into a five-night stay in a psychiatric ward. Alice Stango has since filed a lawsuit against the school district and the county.

It was also writing assignments for English class that got eighth-grader Troy Foley, from the California coastal town of Half Moon Bay, in trouble. In an essay titled "The Riot," Foley, then 14, wrote of a kid who is so enraged with school rules, especially the ones forbidding him to wear a hat and drink soda during class, that he incites a student riot that ends with the principal getting bludgeoned to death. Two weeks later, Foley handed in "Goin' Postal," an equally violent tale about a character named Martin who sneaks a pistol into school and kills a police officer, the vice principal and principal. Though he had no history of violent or even disruptive behavior, Foley was suspended for five days for making a terroristic threat. Foley's mother, assisted by the American Civil Liberties Union, managed to have the record changed to state that Foley was suspended for two days for using profanity in school assignments. Foley has since skipped high school and is enrolled at a two-year community college.

Parents and lawyers of both boys contend that the schools overreacted in these cases, punishing children whose only crime was a vivid imagination. But even if that's so, it leaves an important question unanswered: how do principals and teachers know when a violent story or remark signals a real threat? Those who turn to psychological research will find only equivocal answers at best.

"These things may be indicators, and they may not," says Kevin Dwyer, Ph.D., president-elect of the National Association of School Psychologists. "To try to predict an individual's future behavior based on what they say or write isn't really possible." His view is shared by Edward Taylor, Ph.D., professor of social work at the University of Illinois at Urbana-Champaign and an expert on childhood mental illness. "I don't know of any study that has empirically examined whether the use of violent language in creative writing can actually predict those who are going to commit a crime," declares Taylor. Such language so permeates American popular culture, he notes, that its use doesn't necessarily indicate a predilection for the use of force.

Heightened Security

Mindful of the complexities involved in predicting which students will become violent, many school districts are attempting to circumvent the threat entirely by altering their physical landscapes. Located in the small town of West Paducah, Kentucky, on the banks of the Ohio River, Heath High School was dragged into the national spotlight in the winter of 1997 when 14-year-old Michael Carneal gunned down classmates, killing three girls. The school quickly convened a security committee, which authorized a $148,000 security plan.

Today, Heath requires visitors, teachers and students to wear identification tags around their necks at all times, like soldiers. It has students sign consent forms authorizing staff to rummage through backpacks and cars for weapons; each morning before entering school, students line up to have their bags searched. Heath also has hired a uniformed, armed security guard. Officials have prepared should a weapon slip by security. They've purchased two-way radios for staff members to wear on their belts, in case they need to communicate during an attack. And they've placed emergency medical kits and disaster-instruction manuals in each classroom.

The new environment at Heath High School dismays many parents and students. "They made my son sign papers so they can search his possessions, his locker, anything, anytime," says one unhappy parent. "From what I understand, the Constitution is still in effect. I don't like the idea of my child going to school and having school officials search him at their discretion. They're trying their best, but they don't seem to be getting it right."

Heath's principal Bill Bond defends the measures. "We have restrictions on everything we do," he points out. "I've never thought about carrying a bomb on an airplane, but I pass through airport security just like everybody else. The very concept of security is always going to reduce freedom. That is a trade-off people have been dealing with since the beginning of time."

The Trend Spreads

Schools around the country are following Heath's lead. In April 1998, an Indiana school district became the first in the country to install metal detectors in its elementary schools, after three of its students were caught bringing guns into the buildings. In January 1999, the U.S. Department of Education reported that nearly 6300 students were expelled in the 1996–1997 school year for carrying firearms: 58% had handguns, 7% rifles or shotguns and 35% other weapons, including bombs and grenades.

Faced with such statistics, more schools than ever before are buying security devices like spiked fences, motorized gates and blast-proof metal covers for doors and windows. Administrators are also signing up in droves for the services of security experts. Jesus Villahermosa Jr., a deputy sheriff in Pierce County, Washington, expects to run 65 sessions for educators in 1999, double the number held in 1997. "I'm completely booked," says Villahermosa, whose curriculum includes how to disarm students and how to run lock-down drills.

Such measures may make schools feel less vulnerable, but how do they affect the learning that goes on inside? Here again, research provides only tentative answers. Citing neurological and psychological research, Renate Nummela Caine, professor emeritus of educational psychology at California State University–San Bernadino, maintains that when students feel threatened or helpless, their brains "downshift" into more primitive states, and their ability to think becomes automatic and limited, instinctive rather than creative.

Regimented classrooms, inflexible teachers, an atmosphere of suspicion, can all induce feelings of helplessness, contends Caine, author with her husband Geoffrey Caine, a law professor turned educational specialist, of *Making Connections: Teaching and the Human Brain*. "What schools are doing is creating conditions that are comparable to prisons," she declares. "Where else are people searched every day and watched every minute? They want to clamp down and they want control. It's based on fear, and it's an understandable reaction given the circumstances, but the problem is that they're not looking at other solutions."

Heightened Measures Are Counterproductive

Psychologists say that surrounding troubled young people with the accoutrements of a police state may only fuel their fascination with guns and increase their resistance to authority. Likewise, punishing young people for talking or writing about their violent musings may just force the fantasies underground, where they may grow more exaggerated and extreme. "It's a response that says, 'We don't know how to react, so we're going to respond harshly,'" says Patrick Tolan, Ph.D., professor of adolescent development and intervention at the University of Illinois–Chicago. "If you're a child, would you come forward and say you're troubled in that atmosphere? Are you going to rely on adults if that is how simplistically they think about things? Rather than saying something to a counselor, you might well keep quiet."

Suspending or expelling a student, moreover, strips him of the structure of school and the company of people he knows, perhaps deepening his alienation and driving him to more desperate acts. Kip Kinkel, for example, went on his rampage after being suspended from school for possessing a stolen handgun.

Yet there are punishments more severe and alienating than suspensions and expulsions. As schools begin to resemble police precincts, school officials are abdicating their duty to counsel and discipline unruly students and letting the cops down the hall handle the classroom disruptions, bullying and schoolyard fights. And the cops aren't taking any chances. They're arresting students and feeding them into a criminal justice system that sees little distinction between kids and adults. "Once that police officer is on the scene, the principals and teachers lose control completely," says Vincent Shiraldi, executive director of the Justice Policy Institute in Washington. "I think it will make students a more litigious group and much less able to solve their problems peacefully and reasonably."

A Better Way

There may be a better way, and educators are beginning to look for it. Instead of building schools like fortresses, architects are experimenting with ways to open them up and make them more welcoming. Designers are lowering lockers to waist-height and in some cases eliminating them entirely, so students can't hide behind them or use them as storage spaces for guns. Instead of being built on the outskirts of a school, administrative offices are being placed in the middle, enclosed in glass walls so officials can see what's going on. Gymnasiums and auditoriums are being opened to the public, serving as meeting places for the local chamber of commerce or performing arts group. "The kids feel nurtured by this," says Steven Bingler, a school architect in New Orleans who participated in an October 1998 symposium on making schools safer that was sponsored by the U.S. Department of Education and the White House Millennium Council. "School doesn't feel like a prison to them anymore."

On a more personal level, some schools are offering increased access to counselors; others have hired a "violence prevention coordinator" to whom students can give anonymous tips about classmates in trouble. In accord with this less punitive, more therapeutic approach, students who use threatening language are being steered into anger-management programs, intensive therapy and to other support services.

As for Aaron Leese, he was charged with making a terroristic threat and thrown in a holding cell for the afternoon. "My thought was that they wanted to scare me a bit so that I would bend to the system," he says. The charge was dropped after he submitted to a 90-day probation and a psychiatric evaluation. Leese was ordered to stay off school property, forcing him to miss all the senior activities planned for the end of the year—a banquet, a picnic, a dance. Then his principal, Superintendent Linda Hippert, relented. "I felt that Aaron needed to be punished, but my assumption after the investigation was that the punishment did not fit the crime," says Hippert. "I know Aaron very well, and what he was denied was above and beyond what he had done." With her blessing, Leese was allowed to graduate with his class.

TIGHTER GUN CONTROL LAWS ARE NECESSARY

Hank Kalet

Hank Kalet contends in the following article that restricting gun manufacturing and sales is America's best hope of preventing another school massacre. Kalet writes that America's violent culture helped to create Dylan Klebold and Eric Harris, the two students who killed twelve classmates and one teacher in 1999 at Columbine High School in Littleton, Colorado; however, he argues that restricting First Amendment freedoms and denying artistic expression will do little to stem the flood of violence in American schools. Kalet points out that Klebold and Harris were able to commit their rampage because access to firepower is so easy in America. Limiting the possibility that guns will fall into the hands of teens like Harris and Klebold, Kalet explains, is the only measure that will prevent future tragedies. Kalet is a newspaper editor and poet.

Perhaps it's a cultural thing, violence begetting violence, ending with dead teenagers in the library of a suburban high school. Perhaps we should have expected it, this rash of shootings, the bloodshed.

Perhaps.

But that doesn't mean we shouldn't be outraged, shouldn't demand answers, shouldn't take that difficult look within ourselves.

Even after the shooting in Littleton, Colorado, we seem at sea about what happened. We want to blame music, movies, television, video games, anything but the simple premise that we are a violent culture becoming more and more violent everyday.

This is a story about guns, about brute force, about a culture that respects and demands violence in its everyday interactions. This is the story of American society, played out at a high school in the Midwest. The story of Columbine High School in Littleton, Colorado, of Bethel, Alaska, of Jonesboro, Arkansas, and Wyoming, Delaware. This is the story of kids with guns, of a culture of privilege and power and the powerless and the violent methods we've sanctioned to level the playing fields.

Reprinted from "Violence Strikes Close to Home," by Hank Kalet, *Progressive Populist*, July 1999. Reprinted with permission from the author.

Dylan and Eric

The story of Dylan Klebold and Eric Harris and the shootings at Columbine High School, according to various press reports, begins with a school culture in which the more popular students, the stronger students, the jocks preyed upon the weaker students and outsiders, pushing them into lockers and generally harassing them.

"Jocks pushed them against lockers, yelled 'faggot' and 'loser' at them while they ate lunch in the cafeteria," according to *Rolling Stone*. "One day a few weeks before the killings, Dylan, Eric and Brooks Brown (a friend) were standing out on Pierce Street near the school, having a smoke, when a car full of jocks rolled by. A bottle came flying from the car and shattered at the feet of the three boys."

This is the kind of thing that happens every day at high schools across the country. It is the kind of atmosphere that allowed the teenaged football players in Glen Ridge, New Jersey, to believe they could rape a mentally retarded classmate, that they could perform savage acts upon her, that they could do so with impunity. It is the kind of attitude that allowed members of California's teen-age Spur Posse to play its abusive games of sexual conquest and to view their female victims as little more than collateral damage in their escapades.

The Legacy of the Bully

It is the legacy of the bully, a legacy we seem willing to accept and even endorse, its sinister effects seeping into our political and economic cultures, our films and music and television, our everyday dealings with just about everyone with whom we must interact.

It is visible in the way New York Mayor Rudy Giuliani deals with his critics as he lashes out at protesters and reporters, calling them names, questioning their motives and almost never taking the time to listen to their questions or offer answers. It is visible in the way police departments across the country storm their inner cities as if they were invading superpowers.

It is a Republican Party moving to circumvent the will of the voters during an ugly and divisive impeachment proceeding, a Democratic president bombing Iraq and Serbia, turning to the violent option and abandoning any notion of diplomacy, negotiation or compromise to make his point heard.

It is [businessman] Chainsaw Al Dunlap methodically dismantling companies without regard for the people who work for them, the cities in which they are located or anything other than the quick and dirty profit.

It is the swagger of the professional athlete, the rock and rap star, the pictures of the privileged enjoying privilege on television, in the movies, in music videos.

This is not to excuse the Littleton killers. Dylan Klebold and Eric Harris are the ones who pulled the triggers, are the ones who left 13 people and themselves dead at Columbine High School. They bear the ultimate responsibility.

But there is no doubt in my mind that we helped create the killers that Klebold and Harris were to become.

Not because they listened to Rammstein or KMFDM, or because they played Doom or watched the films of Quentin Tarantino. That would be too easy.

This violent streak is part of our American mythology, is central to the legend we've created about our westward expansion, our growth as a superpower. We believe we always should meet might with might, strength with strength and violence with violence.

John Wayne's strong, silent avenger, Clint Eastwood's no-name gunslinger, Dirty Harry, Rambo, Arnold Schwarzenegger, Jean Claude Van Damme are the products of our dysfunctional imaginations. So are hard-core speed metal and gangsta rap, video games and the panoply of violent entertainments proliferating through our economy. They are not the genesis of our violent culture. They do not create the violence in which our society wallows. They are a reflection of the depth to which violence has become a part of us.

Limit Accessibility to Guns

And when you add easy access to firepower, an ability to buy guns—not just handguns, but assault rifles and all manner of weapons—on the black market or at gun shows, then conflagration almost seems inevitable.

Anywhere.

Which is why it is so scary.

Our best hope is not to impose restrictions on films and music, to scale back the First Amendment or deny artistic or press freedoms. That will do little to stem the violence.

Our best hope is to impose restrictions on the manufacture and distribution of guns, to stop the open sale of fire power at gun shows, to limit the kinds of guns companies can produce, to limit the possibility that weapons can get into the hands of teens like Dylan Klebold and Eric Harris.

TEACHERS SHOULD BE ARMED

Massad Ayoob

In the following selection, Massad Ayoob writes that the stringent gun control measures proposed in the wake of the April
1999 shooting deaths of fifteen people at Columbine High
School in Littleton, Colorado, will not be able to prevent similar
massacres in the future. While Ayoob does advocate a variety of
long-term measures to combat school violence, he argues that
the arming of teachers would have an immediate impact on violent behavior in schools. Ayoob points out that a number of the
high-profile school shootings that have occurred in U.S. schools
since 1996 have been brought to an end by responsible adults
using weapons of their own. Massad Ayoob is the director of the
Lethal Force Institute in Concord, New Hampshire, which trains
police officers and military personnel in self-defense techniques.

The echoes had barely faded from the gunfire at Columbine High
School in Littleton, Colorado, before the gun-control lobby began
shouting for more restrictive laws, a chorus that is sure to grow in the
wake of the shooting in Conyers, Georgia, in which six students were
wounded.

In May 1999 the Senate responded, approving a measure that
would require handguns to be sold with child-safety devices as well as
mandatory background checks for gun sales at gun shows and pawn
shops. What will these bills do to prevent a mass murder like the one
in Colorado? Not much. But one of the few immediate steps that
could stop killers in the school yard is deemed beyond the pale. I'm
referring to arming schoolteachers.

An Absurd Idea?

To many people, that suggestion sounds absurd; gentle molders of
young minds should not carry lethal weapons. Yet there is good prece-
dent for the idea. In Israel armed teachers are common, and terrorist
attacks at schools nonexistent. Indeed, it was only during a 1997 visit
by Israeli schoolgirls to the "Island of Peace" along the Jordanian bor-
der, in which the teachers had been asked to leave their weapons

behind, that an Arab gunman took advantage of an easy opportunity to open fire, killing seven children and wounding another six.

Similar precedents exist in the U.S. In 1997, 16-year-old Luke Woodham entered Pearl High School in Pearl, Mississippi, armed with his estranged father's hunting rifle and dozens of cartridges. When Woodham opened fire, vice principal Joel Myrick sprinted to the parking lot, grabbed a Colt .45 automatic pistol from his truck and forced the gunman to surrender by pointing the gun at his head. In 1998, Andrew Wurst, 14, opened fire on an eighth-grade graduation dance in Edinboro, Pennsylvania. The owner of the banquet hall where the dance was being held grabbed a shotgun from his office and quickly confronted Wurst, who dropped his gun. The toll was thus limited to one slain teacher and two wounded students.

The Columbine massacre brought to eight the number of highly publicized "school shootings" since 1996. Of these, two were brought to an end by responsible adults who had access to weapons of their own. Another two—in Jonesboro, Arkansas [on March 24, 1998, Mitchell Johnson and Andrew Golden killed four classmates and one teacher and wounded ten others at Westside Middle School], and Bethel, Alaska [on February 19, 1997, Evan Ramsey killed one student and the principal at Bethel High School]—ended with no further bloodshed after armed police arrived and confronted the killers at gunpoint. Three more incidents concluded when the perpetrators were forcibly confronted by brave individuals acting without the benefit of a gun. Finally, it should be noted that the Columbine killers turned their guns on themselves almost as soon as they realized a SWAT team was in the building and closing in on them.

Armed Personnel Make a Difference

Those who are aghast at the thought of arming school personnel say that the presence of an armed school officer made no difference in the Littleton tragedy. They are wrong. The officer, a Jefferson County deputy sheriff, engaged the gunmen very early in the shooting. Firing at a distance of some 70 yards (almost three times the range at which police qualify with their pistols), and armed only with a 9mm handgun, the officer was nonetheless able to keep the better-armed killers at bay long enough to reduce the death toll significantly.

It is true, however, that if the school officer had not been initially alone the assailants may well have been more effectively confronted. If, for example, Dave Sanders, the brave teacher who was killed trying to save his students, had been armed and trained, he might have been able to put an end to the violence and save his own life in the bargain.

To be sure, arming school personnel does not by itself guarantee an end to school violence; any long-term solutions must embrace a variety of measures, and not just pat answers such as banning violent movies, video games or guns. But in the near term, trained and responsible adults armed with concealed weapons and likely to be in a position to interdict potential gunmen are in fact a viable solution.

This is not as drastic a measure as it may seem. No school has its own fire-fighting battalion on the grounds, but all adult employees of the school know how to operate fire extinguishers and supervise an orderly fire drill. A school nurse is generally on hand, but virtually all teachers and school administrators have learned basic first aid and CPR. It is but a small step from here to train school personnel in the use of firearms, and to arm at least some of them.

Thorough Testing and Training

For the concept to work, armed teachers would have to be volunteers who pass strict psychological testing, and go through at least as much training in firearms and the judicious use of deadly force as current laws demand of armed security guards. The weapons would have to be discreetly concealed, and which personnel are armed should be revealed only on a need-to-know basis.

Yes, professional educators carrying lethal weapons is probably unthinkable to some. But previously unthinkable dangers can sometimes only be neutralized by previously unthinkable defenses.

ORGANIZATIONS TO CONTACT

The editors have compiled the following list of organizations concerned with the issues presented in this book. The descriptions are derived from materials provided by the organizations. All have publications or information available for interested readers. The list was compiled on the date of publication of the present volume; the information provided here may change. Be aware that many organizations take several weeks or longer to respond to inquiries, so allow as much time as possible.

American Academy of Child and Adolescent Psychiatry (AACAP)
3615 Wisconsin Ave. NW, Washington, DC 20016-3007
(202) 966-7300 • fax: (202) 966-2891
website: http://www.aacap.org

AACAP is the leading national professional medical association committed to treating the seven to twelve million American youth suffering from mental, behavioral, and developmental disorders. It publishes the monthly *Journal of the American Academy of Child and Adolescent Psychiatry* and the reports "Children and TV Violence," "Understanding Violent Behavior in Children and Adolescents," and "Children's Threats: When Are They Serious?"

American Civil Liberties Union (ACLU)
125 Broad St., 18th Fl., New York, NY 10004
(212) 549-2500 • fax: (212) 549-2646
website: http://www.aclu.org

The ACLU is a national organization that works to defend Americans' civil rights as guaranteed by the U.S. Constitution. It works to establish equality before the law, regardless of race, color, sexual orientation, or national origin. The ACLU publishes and distributes the semiannual newsletter *Civil Liberties Alert*, policy statements, pamphlets, and reports which include "From Words to Weapons: The Violence Surrounding Our Schools."

Canadians Concerned About Violence in Entertainment (C-CAVE)
167 Glen Rd., Toronto, ON M4W 2W8 Canada
(416) 961-0853 • fax: (416) 929-2720
e-mail: rdyson@oise.utoronto.ca

C-CAVE conducts research on the harmful effects violence in the media has on society and provides its findings to the Canadian government and public. The organization's committees research issues of violence against women and children, sports violence, and pornography. C-CAVE disseminates educational materials, including periodic news updates.

Center for the Prevention of School Violence
20 Enterprise St., Ste. 2, Raleigh, NC 27607-7375
(800) 299-6054 • (919) 515-9397 • fax: (919) 515-9561
e-mail: joanne_mcdaniel@ncsu.edu
website: http://www2.ncsu.edu/ncsu/cep/PreViolence

The Center for the Prevention of School Violence is a primary point of contact for information, programs, and research about school violence and its prevention. As a clearinghouse, it provides information about all aspects of the problems which fall under the heading of school violence as well as information about strategies that are directed at solving these problems.

Mediascope
12711 Ventura Blvd., Ste. 440, Studio City, CA 91604
(818) 508-2080 • fax: (808) 508-2088
e-mail: facts@mediascope.org • website: http://www.mediascope.org

Mediascope is a national, nonprofit research and public policy organization working to raise awareness about the way media affects society. Founded in 1992, it encourages responsible depictions of social and health issues in film, television, the Internet, video games, advertising, and music. Among its many publications are *The Social Effects of Electronic Interactive Games: An Annotated Bibliography*, *National Television Violence Study*, and *How Children Process Television*.

Morality in Media (MIM)
475 Riverside Dr., Ste. 239, New York, NY 10115
(212) 870-3222 • fax: (212) 870-2765
e-mail: mimnyc@ix.netcom.com
website: http://www.netcom.com/~mimnyc/index.html

Established in 1962, MIM is a national, not-for-profit interfaith organization that works to combat obscenity and violence and to uphold decency standards in the media. It maintains the National Obscenity Law Center, a clearinghouse of legal materials, and conducts public information programs to involve concerned citizens. Its publications include the bimonthly *Morality in Media* newsletter and the handbook *TV: The World's Greatest Mind-Bender*.

National Alliance for Safe Schools (NASS)
PO Box 290, Slanesville, WV 25445
(888) 510-6500 • (304) 496-8100 • fax: (304) 496-8105
e-mail: nass@raven-villages.net • website: http://www.safeschools.org

Founded in 1977 by a group of school security directors, the National Alliance for Safe Schools was established to provide training, security assessments, and technical assistance to school districts interested in reducing school-based crime and violence. It publishes the book *Making Schools Safe for Students*.

National Association of School Resource Officers (NASRO)
PO Box 40, Boynton Beach, FL 33425-0040
(888) 316-2776
e-mail: resourcer@aol.com • website: http://www.nasro.org

The National Association of School Resource Officers is the first and only nonprofit training organization made up of liaison officers currently assigned to a school community. Its mission is to break down the barriers between law enforcement and youth by establishing better communication about the legal system. Its official publication is *Resourcer*.

National Institute of Justice (NIJ)
National Criminal Justice Reference Service (NCJRS)
PO Box 6000 Rockville, MD 20849-6000
(800) 851-3420 • (301) 519-5500
e-mail: askncjrs@ncjrs.org • website: http://www.ncjrs.org

A component of the Office of Justice Programs of the U.S. Department of Justice, the NIJ supports research on crime, criminal behavior, and crime prevention. The National Criminal Justice Reference Service acts as a clearinghouse for criminal justice information for researchers and other interested individuals. Among the numerous reports it publishes and distributes are "Serious and Violent Juvenile Offenders," "Adolescent Violence: A View from the Street," and "Partnerships to Prevent Youth Violence."

National School Safety Center (NSSC)
141 Duesenberg Dr., Ste. 11, Westlake Village, CA 91362
(805) 373-9977 • fax: (805) 373-9277
e-mail: info@nssc1.org • website: http://nssc1.org

The NSSC is a research organization that studies school crime and violence, including hate crimes. The center's mandate is to focus national attention on cooperative solutions to problems which disrupt the educational process. NSSC provides training, technical assistance, legal and legislative aid, and publications and films toward this cause. Its resources include the books *Set Straight on Bullies* and *Gangs in Schools: Breaking Up Is Hard to Do* and the newsletter, *School Safety Update*, which is published nine times a year.

Office of Juvenile Justice and Delinquency Prevention (OJJDP)
810 Seventh St. NW, Washington, DC 20531
(202) 307-5911 • fax: (202) 307-2093
e-mail: askjj@ojp.usdoj.gov • website: http://ojjdp.ncjrs.org

As the primary federal agency charged with monitoring and improving the juvenile justice system, the OJJDP develops and funds programs on juvenile justice. Among its goals are the prevention and control of illegal drug use and serious crime by juveniles. Through its Juvenile Justice Clearinghouse, the OJJDP distributes fact sheets and reports such as "How Juveniles Get to Criminal Court," "Gang Suppression and Intervention: Community Models," and "Minorities and the Juvenile Justice System."

The Oregon Social Learning Center (OSLC)
160 E. 4th Ave., Eugene, OR 97401
(541) 485-2711 • fax: (541) 485-7087
website: http://www.oslc.org

OSLC is a nonprofit, independent research center dedicated to finding ways to help children and parents as they cope with daily problems. The center is known for its successful work in designing and implementing interventions for children and parents to help encourage successful adjustment and to discourage aggressive behaviors within the family, the school, and the community. OSLC has published over 400 articles in scientific journals, written over 200 chapters in textbooks about children and adolescents and their families, published eleven books, and made many films, videotapes, and audiotapes on parenting.

The Parent Project, Inc.
2848 Longhorn St., Ontario, CA 91761
(800) 372-8886 • fax: (909) 923-7372
e-mail: training@parentproject.com • website: http://www.parentproject.com

The Parent Project is an award-winning model for school and community programs serving high-risk families. Focusing on the most destructive of adolescent behaviors, the Parent Project's training program, *A Parent's Guide to Changing Destructive Adolescent Behavior*, offers no-nonsense solutions to the serious problems parents face raising children in today's world.

Partners Against Violence Network (PAVNET) Online
(301) 504-5462
e-mail: jgladsto@nalusda.gov • website: http://www.pavnet.org

PAVNET Online is a virtual library of information about violence and youth-at-risk, representing data from seven different federal agencies. Its programs promote the prevention of youth violence through education as well as through sports and recreation. Among PAVNET's curricula publications are *Creative Conflict Solving for Kids* and *Escalating Violence: The Impact of Peers*. The monthly *PAVNET Online* newsletter is also available at its website.

Safe Schools and Violence Prevention Office (SSVPO)
660 J St., Suite 400, Sacramento, CA 95814
(916) 323-2183 • fax: (916) 323-6061
website: http://www.cde.ca.gov/spbranch/safety/safetyhome.html

Operated by the California Department of Education, SSVPO offers assistance, training, materials, as well as supporting grant programs to foster the development of safe schools and communities. Its programs include counseling and guidance, conflict resolution and youth mediation, hate-motivated behavior violence prevention, high-risk youth education, gang risk intervention, and school/law enforcement partnership. SSVPO's publications include *Safe Schools: A Planning Guide for Action, On Alert: Gang Prevention—School In-Service Guidelines,* and *Hate-Motivated Behavior in Schools.*

U.S. Department of Education
Safe and Drug-Free Schools Program
400 Maryland Ave. SW, Washington, DC 20202
(800) USA-LEARN • (202) 260-3954 • fax: (202) 401-0689
e-mail: customerservice@inet.ed.gov • website: http://www.ed.gov

The Safe and Drug-Free Schools Program is the U.S. Department of Education's primary vehicle for reducing drug, alcohol and tobacco use, and violence, through education and prevention activities in our nation's schools. It publishes the reports "Student Victimization at School," "Indicators of School Crime and Safety," and "Early Warning, Timely Response: A Guide to Safe Schools."

Youth Crime Watch of America (YCWA)
9300 S. Dadeland Blvd., Suite 100, Miami, FL 33156
(305) 670-2409 • fax: (305) 670-3805
e-mail: ycwa@ycwa.org • website: http://www.ycwa.org

Youth Crime Watch of America is a nonprofit organization that assists youth in actively reducing crime and drug use in their schools and communities. Its resources include handbooks for adult advisors and youth on starting and operating a Youth Crime Watch program, a *Getting Started* video, a *Mentoring Activities* handbook, and a *Talking with Youth About Prevention* teaching guide.

BIBLIOGRAPHY

Books

Carl W. Bosch   *Schools Under Siege: Guns, Gangs and Hidden Dangers.* Springfield, NJ: Enslow, 1997.

Vic Cox   *Guns, Violence and Teens.* Springfield, NJ: Enslow, 1997.

Gordon A. Crews   *The Evolution of School Disturbance in America.*
and M. Reid Counts   Westport, CT: Praeger, 1997.

Richard L. Curwin   *As Tough as Necessary: Countering Violence, Aggression,*
and Allen N. Mendler   *and Hostility in Our Schools.* Alexandria, VA: Association for Supervision and Curriculum Development, 1997.

John Devine   *Maximum Security: The Culture of Violence in Inner-City Schools.* Chicago: University of Chicago Press, 1996.

Margaret Dolan   *School Violence...Calming the Storm: A Guide to Creating a Fight-Free School Environment.* Marietta, GA: Rising Sun, 1998.

Suellen Fried and   *Bullies and Victims: Helping Your Child Survive the*
Paula Fried   *Schoolyard Battlefield.* New York: M. Evans, 1998.

Arnold P. Goldstein,   *Student Aggression: Prevention, Management, and*
Berj Harootunian,   *Replacement Training.* New York: Guilford Press, 1999.
and Jane Conoley

Arnold P. Goldstein   *Gangs in Schools: Signs, Symbols, and Solutions.*
and Donald W.   Champaign, IL: Research Press, 1998.
Kodluboy

Richard Lawrence   *School Crime and Juvenile Justice.* New York: Oxford University Press, 1997.

Maryann Miller   *Coping with Weapons and Violence in School and on Your Street.* New York: Rosen, 1999.

Periodicals

Jerry Adler and   "How to Fight Back," *Newsweek,* May 3, 1999.
Karen Springen

Timothy C. Brennan Jr.   "Uneasy Days for Schools," *Newsweek,* June 29, 1998.

Nancy D. Brenner,   "Recent Trends in Violence-Related Behaviors Among
Thomas R. Simon,   High School Students in the United States," *JAMA,*
Etienne G. Krug,   August 4, 1999. Available from 515 N. State St.,
and Richard Lowry   Chicago, IL 60610.

John Cloud   "Just a Routine School Shooting," *Time,* May 31, 1999.

Barbara Dority   "Big Brother Goes to High School," *Humanist,* March/April 1997.

Carey Goldberg   "For Those Who Dress Differently, an Increase in Being Viewed as Abnormal," *New York Times,* May 1, 1999.

S.C. Gwynne	"Is Anyplace Safe?" *Time*, August 23, 1999.
Evelyn Larrubia and Richard O'Reilly	"When Guns Are Brought to School," *Los Angeles Times*, July 4, 1999.
David L. Marcus	"Metal Detectors Alone Can't Guarantee Safety," *U.S. News & World Report*, May 3, 1999.
Lawrie Mifflin	"Many Researchers Say Link Is Already Clear on Media and Youth Violence," *New York Times*, May 9, 1999.
Anna Mulrine	"Once Bullied, Now Bullies—with Guns," *U.S. News & World Report*, May 3, 1999.
Cheryl K. Olson	"Making School Safe," *Parents*, November 1997.
Camille Paglia	"Why School?" *Interview*, July 1999.
Kevin Sack	"Schools Add Security and Tighten Dress, Speech and Civility Rules," *New York Times*, May 24, 1999.
Russell J. Skiba and Reece L. Peterson	"The Dark Side of Zero Tolerance: Can Punishment Lead to Safe Schools?" *Phi Delta Kappan*, January 1999.
Abigail Thernstrom	"Courting Disorder in the Schools," *Public Interest*, Summer 1999.
Jackson Toby	"Getting Serious About School Discipline," *Public Interest*, Fall 1998.
Amy Wallace and Faye Fiore	"Hollywood Surprised by Clinton's Violence Inquiry," *Los Angeles Times*, June 7, 1999.
Patrick Welsh	"The Price of Protection," *U.S. News & World Report*, May 3, 1999.
Peter Wilkinson and Matt Hendrickson	"Humiliation and Revenge," *Rolling Stone*, June 10, 1999.

INDEX